DECORATIVE EGGS

DECORATIVE EGGS

CANDACE ORD MANROE

CRESCENT BOOKS
New York

Principal photography by John Gruen and Richard Todd

A FRIEDMAN GROUP BOOK

This 1992 edition published by Crescent Books, distributed by Outlet Book Company, Inc., a Random House Company, 225 Park Avenue South, New York, New York 10003.

ISBN 0-517-06032-9

Library of Congress Cataloging-in-Publication Data

Manroe, Candace Ord, 1954–
  Decorative eggs / Candace Ord Manroe.
    p.   cm.
  "A Friedman Group book"—T.p. verso.
  Includes index.
  ISBN 0-517-06032-9 : $14.99
  1. Egg decoration—History.   I. Title.
  TT896.7.M38   1992
  745.594'4—dc20   91-31330
                                                                 CIP

DECORATIVE EGGS
was prepared and produced by
Michael Friedman Publishing Group, Inc.
15 West 26th Street
New York, New York 10010

Editor: Elizabeth Viscott Sullivan
Art Direction: Devorah Levinrad
Designer: Kingsley Parker
Photography Editor: Ede Rothaus

Typeset by Bookworks Plus
Color separation by Scantrans Pte. Ltd.
Printed and bound in Hong Kong by Leefung-Asco Printers Ltd.

8 7 6 5 4 3 2 1

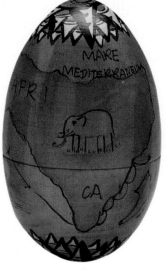

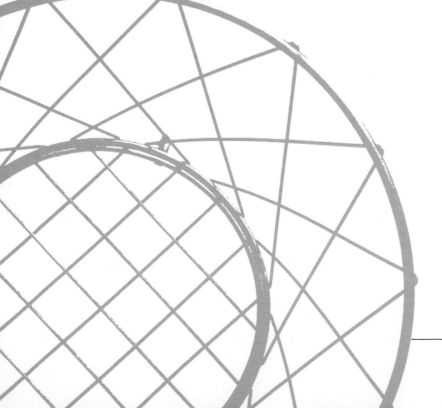

DEDICATION

To my parents, for inspiring an appreciation of art, aesthetics, and traditions; and to Meagan and Drew, the next generation, for making the continuum of tradition a privilege, not labor, of love.

ACKNOWLEDGMENTS

Special thanks to LaDawn Smith for her assistance and research.

Thanks also to George and Vera Hillinger of Los Angeles for their generosity in sharing their unique collection; Maria Schust and the staff of the Ukrainian Museum in New York for their time and expertise; Gwen and Perm Everett and Lee Gelfond Chocolate, Inc., Beverly Hills, and Edelweiss Chocolates, Beverly Hills; Perugina Chocolates and Confection, Inc.; and to the Forbes Magazine Collection, New York.

CONTENTS

CONTENTS

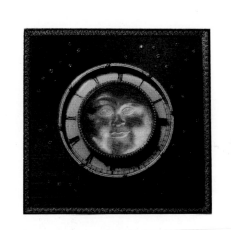

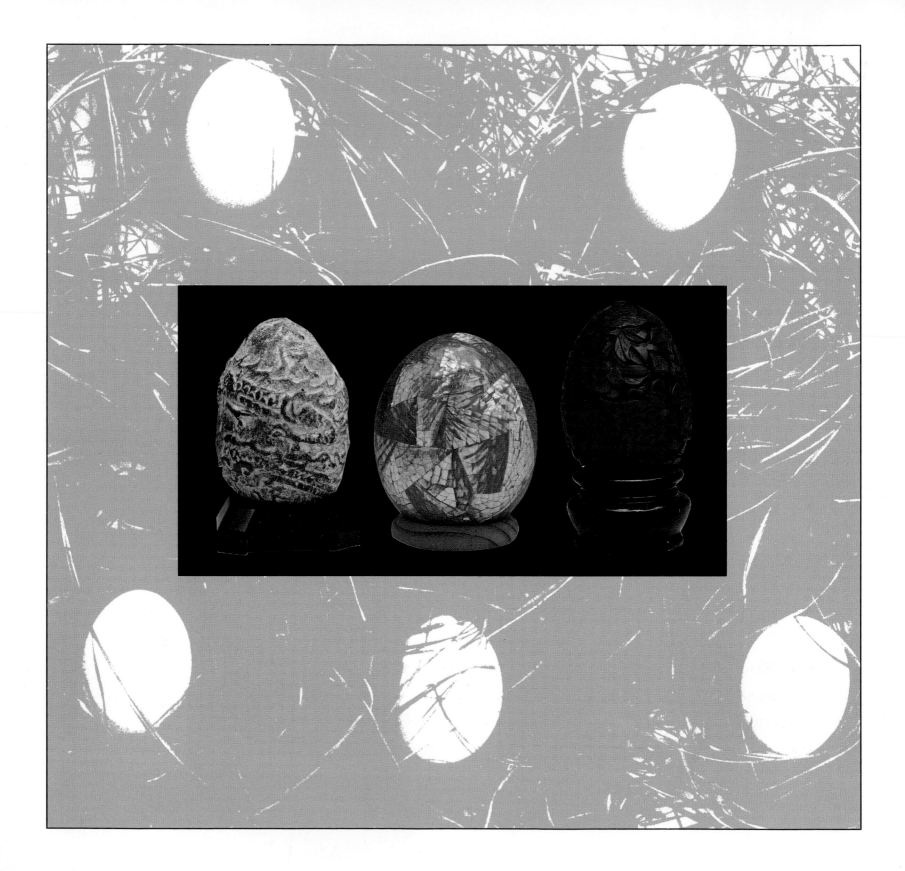

MYTHOLOGY AND MAGIC

Before the world's major religions evolved, segregating societies along theological lines, virtually every early culture had at least one object of faith in common: the egg. Just as all peoples, whether in Mesopotamia or North America, gazed at the sun and stars and imbued those celestial orbs with special meaning, so did they observe the egg and its miraculous role in issuing forth new life. Little wonder the egg figures so centrally in earliest mythology and magic; little wonder it continues today to be a significant symbol for articles of faith; little wonder the humble egg is honored with artistic attention, serving throughout the centuries as one of the most pervasive mediums for creative expression within the decorative arts.

As an important element in mythology, the egg is universal, appearing spontaneously in the lore of otherwise disparate cultures across the globe. To primitive man, the egg represented both new life and the promise of spring. Consequently, few other objects were ascribed such vast, mystical powers. Early man associated the egg with storms, rain, thunder, lightning, solar eclipses, and, of course, fertility. This tradition of attributing symbolic meaning to the unadorned egg has been handed down to the decorative egg — both an art and a folk-art form rife with meaning.

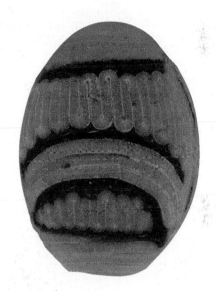

Associated with man's earliest creation myths and believed to possess magical powers, eggs remain one of the decorative arts' most popular mediums. Appliqué, such as this Polish egg adorned with bulrush, is a decorating technique with universal appeal. From the collection of Frances Drwal.

Creation Myths

The Egg and Water

The egg is central in primal mythology worldwide and figures in numerous creation myths, many of which indelibly link it with water. In China in the sixth century B.C., the egg was believed to be responsible for the creation of the earth itself; this ancient legend has it that an egg swam from waters, forming dry land from their depths. Chinese mythology also says that the first man was hatched from an egg dropped from heaven to float on the primordial waters.

The egg as a procreator that ascended from water is found in other cultures' mythology, too. In North America, the Navajos believed that one of their most sacred figures, the Great Coyote Who Was Formed in the Water, hatched from an egg. Similarly, in Peru an early myth held that a great flood covered the earth and, once it receded, left behind five eggs on a mountaintop. From one of these eggs, the august Inca hero, Paricaca, was born.

Egypt has its own myth coupling the life-giving egg with water. In this case, a clump of mud from the Nile River was transformed into the world egg — that is, the universe itself, with a yet-unformed mass like the early embryo just developing within an eggshell — by the god of creation. The metamorphosis occurred on a potter's wheel, and the egg rendered forth was of gold, not clay.

Interestingly, this idea of a world egg was not confined to the banks of the Nile. In one region of Finland, inhabitants credited the egg with the creation of the world.

The Hindus also shared a belief in the world egg. Their legend says the world originated from the "waters of chaos." From here, a golden world egg

Appearing spontaneously as an art form in different ancient cultures, decorative eggs reflect the heritage of their makers, as shown by these ceramic and sculpture Zuni eggs (left and below, left), and this exuberant folk-art wooden egg from Romania (below, right).

was formed, which in turn hatched Prajapati, the father of gods and of all living creatures.

With some modification, the world-egg myth was exerting influence in Europe as late as the Middle Ages, when it was believed that the earth was, in fact, an egg. Europeans believed that within the egg's "yolk," metals grew, in much the same way that an embryo develops.

Not as comprehensive as the world-egg myth, a Polynesian legend tells that the big island of Hawaii was laid like an egg by a huge bird at a time when there was no other existing land.

That eggs were revered in prehistoric time is evidenced by the presence of clay eggs discovered in prehistoric tombs in both Russia and Sweden. After the introduction of writing, claims attributing supernatural powers to the egg were no longer circulated solely via the oral tradition. Egyptian scrolls dating as far back as 1580 to 1085 B.C. provide the first written documentation of the egg's significance. According to the scrolls, the egg is a mighty deity who presides over the moon, lakes, and islands and is, in fact, a direct gift from the sun.

The Egg and the Sun

Like Egypt, other cultures' mythology also pairs the egg with the sun. An Indian myth so closely linked the two that magical rites enlisted the egg to magnify the radiation of the sun's rays. In the Ukraine, which has a long tradition of producing some of the world's most flamboyant and beautiful decorative eggs, the egg originally symbolized the sun. This pagan meaning was adapted easily after the introduction of Christianity, which holds Christ as the light or sun of the world. The term *Easter*, in fact, means "dawn" or "the season of the rising sun." Decorative Easter eggs, then, though now ascribed Christian meaning, continue the pagans' symbolic association of the egg and the sun.

In his epic poem *Kalevala*, the Finnish writer Elias Lonnrot presented a creation myth in which not only the sun but the earth, moon, sky, and clouds all were formed from the broken eggs of a teal (duck) sent by the high god Ukhor to rest at the knee of the Water Mother.

Divinities

In addition to the egg's role in creation myths and its connection with both the water and the sun, many cultures' mythology includes stories of divinities or heroic figures hatching from eggs. In addition to the aforementioned legends of such hatchings from the Navajos, the Incas, and the Hindus, the revered Miao scribe Mi Wang Sen of Indochina was said to have been born from an egg laid by a pigeon and hatched by a dove. Another important Miao character, the Amazon warrior Mma Ngao Mi, who led her people in battle against the Chinese, was believed to have hatched from a grasshopper egg.

Decorative eggs often are a microcosm of a culture's decorative arts heritage. The bronze egg (opposite) is from Thailand—a land known for its bronze art; the Chinese egg with a Tibetan image (right) is decorated with cloisonné, which is pervasive in that culture.

Magic

Just as the egg was a focal point in mythology, so was it an equally central part of the magical rites practiced by superstitious peoples; some of these rites were practiced into the twentieth century. The egg was seen as providing protection against innumerable evil spirits and catastrophic natural phenomena, sickness and death, accidents, and assorted misfortunes. The tendency to project magical powers upon the egg wasn't confined to the peasant class or to pagan times, either. Eggs as protective charms were present not only in peasant huts, but in the royal palaces and fine quarters of nobility. Eggs figured into the superstitious and mystical rites not only of primitive people, but of cultured Egyptians,

The ceramic egg shown here emanates from the Native American culture, whose mythology had some of its greatest heroes hatching from eggs.

Greeks, Chinese, and Persians. In the Middle Ages, the inclusion of an ostrich egg or goose egg in a decorative display was commonplace within a holy cathedral.

As primitive cultures were forced to become more civilized, the early practice of blood sacrifices of persons or animals as an effective ward against evil was abandoned—but in letter only. Because the egg was by now perceived as a primary symbol for life, containing within its embryo the seeds of the future, it enabled the spirit of blood sacrifices to continue. The egg simply was offered in place of a live sacrifice in some countries to keep trouble at bay; as a vicarious human sacrifice, the egg was believed to be an appropriate offering to evil spirits. The Germans, for example, left eggs out at night to scare away the bad night spirit and the treachery of witches.

Elsewhere, Gypsies buried eggs on the banks of rising streams to appease the floodwaters. The French put an offering of eggs, along with bread and cheese, in their wells to placate the waters into continually flowing. Even into the twentieth century in Bombay, the Indians still constructed some of their buildings' foundations with eggs and milk because they believed they were protective potions.

Krashanky (see chapter 4), single-color, dyed Ukrainian eggs, were believed to be a sure cure for blood poisoning: With a single touch of the egg, the malady would vanish. Similarly, after the introduction of Christianity, the Ukrainians believed that an egg blessed on Easter could be hung about the neck of a seriously ill person to divert the disease from that person into the egg by an almost magnetic supernatural power.

Red eggs were believed to possess especially potent magical powers in many cultures. This red lacquered egg hails from Taiwan.

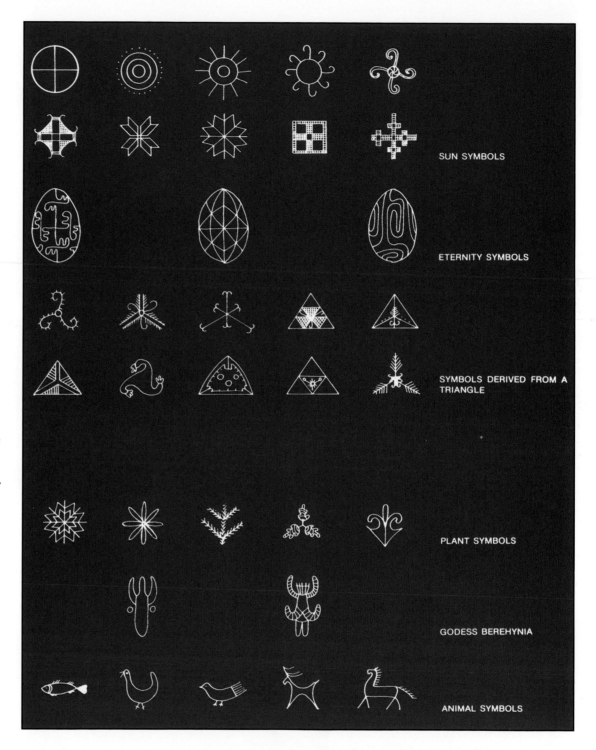

Ukrainian pysanky eggs may be decorated with a variety of design motifs, each of which has particular significance within the culture.

Eggs bearing a design of wheat, a common symbol found from pagan through present times on Ukrainian wax-resist decorated eggs known as *pysanky* (see chapter 4), were lodged in the fields in two locations — at the beginning of the first furrow and at the end of the last — to protect the crops and ensure a bountiful harvest. A modified version of this custom was practiced by the Lithuanians, who continued to believe in the egg's powers even into the twentieth century.

In the Ukraine, different decorative motifs on eggs symbolized different magical powers. Should a Ukrainian couple have no children, for example, the man might be given eggs adorned with designs of roosters and oak leaves to achieve virility.

Perhaps most telling of the Ukrainians' belief in the mystical powers of the egg is their legend regarding the devastating consequences should the tradition of pysanky ever cease: An ancient, vicious monster shackled to an enormous cliff will be freed to roam the entire earth and annihilate all who inhabit it. According to the legend, the monster's servant traverses the globe, keeping a watchful eye on the level of pysanky production. Should the servant discover a slack in the creation of the decorative eggs, he will loosen the monster's chain, allowing evil to course through the world.

Belief in the egg's magical powers extended from eastern Europe to western and northern Europe as well. An Italian legend recounts that a fairy demanded the death of a young girl each year — but with the fortunate stipulation that the weapon be a particular egg found in a seven-headed tiger.

Two legends similar to one another not only accredit the egg with mystical qualities, they presage today's controversial pro-life/pro-choice debate over the inception of "life." The two legends, one Celtic and one Russian, proclaim the existence of souls within eggs.

Both in secular and religious life, the egg was construed as a resource leading to riches. In alchemy, lead purportedly would be transformed into gold when heated in a furnace in an egg-shaped vessel called an aludel. The lead eventually would "hatch" the philosopher's stone, which could turn the lead to gold at a touch. An early Christian myth declared that an egg laid on Good Friday would turn into a diamond if retained for one hundred years.

Mutant or malformed eggs inspired even more superstitions than normal or decorated eggs. In England, eggs not containing a yolk were considered bad luck if brought indoors. In Europe, malformed eggs were believed to be unlucky; if tossed backward behind the home, however, the eggs' spells could be broken and a streak of ill luck averted. In Hungary, a soft-shell egg from a black hen was immediately crushed, for its very existence meant impending death for a family member. In Madagascar, the notion of a mutant egg portending death was narrowed, applying only to pregnant women. If a pregnant woman ate such an egg, it was believed that she would abort her fetus and be left infertile.

Red Eggs

Cross-culturally, one type of egg in particular was believed to possess especially potent powers: the red egg. Red-dyed eggs are both one of the earliest and most pervasive of all decorative eggs. In contemporary times, William Butler Yeats addressed the mystical power of the color red: "Red is the color of magic in every country, and has been so from the very earliest time." An ancient Roman legend bears out Yeats's statement from *Fairy and Folk Tales of the Irish Peasantry*: the birth of the mighty Emperor Alexander Severus coincided with a hen laying a red egg, at which time a prophet foretold of the new baby's grand future.

Its ruddy color evoking images of good health and, in turn, life and fertility, the red egg was often used as an instrument to grant deep-felt desires for these

Symmetrically ornamented with finials, this Chinese cloisonné egg (opposite) projects a beautifully balanced presence that is only appropriate for an object believed to have mystical powers.

things. In France, red eggs were offered to guarantee a hearty crop. In China, red-dyed eggs were offered to the god and goddess of the bed—minor household gods who protected the bedchamber and prevented babies from rolling off the beds. Another Chinese tradition hailed the birth of a male child with red eggs—sometimes, as many as five hundred were offered as thanks to the fertility goddess Tin Hau.

Akin to the Ukrainian legend of the monster and pysanky, Transylvanian lore depicts the Antichrist gnawing at a heavy iron chain, which he manages to eat almost through by Easter. But at that time, he spies the red-dyed eggs of Easter and is distracted long enough for the chain to magically regenerate itself. This legend inspired the saying that when Christians cease to dye red eggs, the world will come to an end.

In a Korean tale, a red egg means more than the continuation of life: It is actually the receptacle for life. The tale portrays the citizens of Chinhan huddling about a white horse bowing to the ground. The horse flies away, leaving behind a red egg, from which is hatched a radiant boy. The intensity of his illumination causes even the sun and moon to increase their brilliance. The Koreans named the child Hyokkose, or "brightness," and he fulfilled their expectations for truly brilliant leadership, becoming the first king of Silla.

But just as the color red can symbolize rosy good health and vibrant life, it also can represent blood. Countless Christian legends take this second meaning to explain the significance of red eggs in that faith.

In a Yugoslavian legend, at Easter the Virgin Mary passed out red eggs that she had colored to remind the world of the saving, sacrificial blood of her son. The legend explains, of course, the origin of the custom of exchanging colored eggs at Easter — a custom that actually predates Christianity, originating with pagan celebrations of spring.

A Romanian legend is even more dramatic. It holds that Mary offered a basket of eggs to soldiers guarding the cross in an effort to make them take pity on Christ. The soldiers dismissed Mary's pleas, but left the basket of eggs at the foot of the cross. The blood of Jesus flowed down from the cross, staining the eggs, thus setting the precedent for the subsequent symbolically colored red Easter egg.

The egg has long been imbued with symbolic meaning and supernatural power. From early mythology and magic on to modern times, the diverse examples of decorative eggs are much more than ornamental. More than objets d'art or craft for its own sake, they are rooted in tradition, vehicles for expressing man's efforts to make sense of life's fundamental questions.

This ceramic Zuni egg (above), whose design motif is suggestive of a spiral seashell, has contemporary appeal in its graphic abstraction.

Decorative eggs evolved in disparate cultures, and there was an overlap in the materials from which they were made. The French egg (opposite, far left) is made from mother-of-pearl and wood, and the American egg pictured beside it also is crafted from an abalone shell.

THE ORIGINS AND EVOLUTION OF THE DECORATIVE EGG

From Pagan to Protestant Traditions

The first people to exchange decorative eggs were the ancient Persians. As symbols of the renewal of life and rebirth, eggs were prized by these people, who festively dyed and exchanged them in conjunction with the spring equinox — the onset of their new year.

Like Persia, pagan Germany and Switzerland used eggs in their customs celebrating spring. Although these people did not decorate eggs, they used them in a decorative fashion, festooning them on decorated, beribboned branches, thus establishing the custom of egg trees even prior to Christianity and its attendant Easter egg customs.

Eastern Europe was host to some of the most intricately decorated eggs, also predating Christianity. The eastern European region best known for elevating the egg to a vibrant folk-art form was the Ukraine. Ukrainian scratch-

Eastern Europe gave rise to some of the world's most inspiring folk-art eggs. These appliquéd bead eggs are from the Bakowena region of Romania.

carved and wax-resist decorative eggs were too noticeable and copious to remain within a contained geographical area. Consequently, similar egg-decorating techniques were employed by neighboring peoples, including the Lithuanians, Polish, and Hungarians, all of whom adapted the techniques to express design motifs with symbolic significance uniquely their own.

The oldest painted eggs from Poland predate the eleventh century and were found upon excavating a Polish castle built at that time. The castle, located in the Opole Wood, Silesia, was erected during a period of strong Slavic influence in that area, just before German influence became predominant. The thirteenth-century writings of Archbishop Vincent Kadlubek state that "in distant times the Poles used to amuse themselves at the expense of their lords with colored eggs."

German poet Freidanck's reference in 1216 in his poem, *"Bescheidenheit,"* to eggs colored red and black reveals that egg decorating had spread to western Europe by that time. Household records of Edward I from 1290 provide the earliest documentation of the egg-decorating custom in England: One logged expense was for the purchase of 450 gold-leafed eggs, which were to be presented as gifts (presumably for Easter) to the royal entourage. In Italy, nuns living near Rome in the 1700s were known to be dying eggs solid colors — red, purple, blue, and yellow — for use in religious ceremonies in which they were blessed and sprinkled with holy water.

The first country to have merged the egg-decorating tradition with the Christian celebration of Easter wasn't Italy, however, but Macedonia. The Macedonian custom was practiced primarily by children, who gathered to dye eggs — mainly the pervasive red, but also some green and yellow ones — and then to sell them at the marketplace. That the already-established custom of decorating eggs was adopted by Christians and interlaid with religious significance is not hard to understand: St. Augustine compared the egg to the hope of eternal life—both represent potential. Colored eggs seemed to appear wherever Christianity spread, and were even found in the artifacts of a Muslim African tribe that once, long ago, was Christian.

Practitioners of the Eastern Orthodox faith exchanged colored eggs on Easter day as a symbol of Christ's resurrection, which represented a new, eternal life free of the shackling confines of physical, earthly death. During religious services in the Middle Ages, they also placed colored eggs in the symbolic tomb of Christ. These eggs were decorated with dyes, and some were embellished with gold, silver, and precious stones. Throughout the centuries, Eastern Orthodox believers exchanged red-dyed eggs on Easter morning and greeted each other by saying, "Christ is risen."

Catholicism prepared the groundwork for the egg-decorating custom long before the nuns in Italy were known to be practicing it. In the fourth century, eggs became an entrenched part of church life, and were presented in services to be sprinkled with holy water and blessed. The Catholic blessing was as follows: "We beseech thee, O Lord, to bestow thy benign blessings upon these eggs, to make them a wholesome food for thy faithful, who gratefully partake of them in honor of the Resurrection of our Lord Jesus Christ." By the twelfth century, eggs had officially entered church creed with the Bendicto Ovorum, which authorized the special use of eggs on the holy days of Easter.

But the Catholics' popularization of the egg in church services didn't spread to Protestant faiths. Pope Paul V's sanctioned ritual for consecrating eggs was swiftly abandoned when England broke from Catholicism and established its own church. Consequently, egg decorating itself fell some in popularity. The

In Poland, the ancient eastern European tradition of egg decorating was continued after Christianity was introduced, resulting in colorfully ornamented Easter eggs.

early American colonists, the majority of whom were Protestant, therefore did not bring with them to this country too strong a tradition of egg decorating — at least not when compared to other cultures, such as Catholic Poland or the Ukraine. This does not mean, however, that America did not eventually develop its own Easter celebrations, which included the decorating of eggs. Eggs were dyed using natural materials (and later, chemical dyes) and were then hidden by adults for Easter egg hunts for children.

Colorful Customs

Despite the abandonment of significant egg decorating in England after its break from Catholicism, the vast majority of the Christian world continued to practice, refine, and expand customs involving the use and decoration of eggs. Although disparate cultures held in common the practice of decorating eggs and associating them with religious celebration, the similarities were fairly superficial; real distinctions appeared in the nuances.

Since the time of Christ, the egg has come into its own as a central element of celebration. In Christian countries throughout the world, Easter is observed with egg races, hunts, and other egg games such as egg rolls and tosses—all primarily for the enjoyment of children.

On Easter Sunday, the Irish eat as many eggs as possible — a minimum of four or five, and some people put away a dozen or more. Adults give eggs to those most in need, sharing both their bounty and religious convictions at once.

In neighboring Wales, Scotland, and England, decorated eggs are more the domain of children, and are collected and utilized in a number of games. For Welsh children, the central activity is called egg begging and is similar to America's Halloween trick-or-treating. The event in Wales is called *clapio wyau*, and its name is derived from the custom of the children clapping two slates together like castanets and singing, "Clap, clap, ask for an egg, small boys in the parish."

English children also go door to door begging for eggs the week before Easter, in what is known as pace egging. Pace eggs — the traditional English Easter eggs — are decorated with the patterns formed by fresh flowers, plants, or herbs that are pressed against the eggshell and held in place by old, different-colored scrap sewing fabrics, which, in turn, are made fast by a tie of linen or other material. The egg is boiled for half an hour, during which time the colored fabrics tint the egg and leave behind the outline of the flowers. The custom of making pace eggs was nearly lost over time, usurped by chocolate and confectionery eggs. But thanks to a few devoted practitioners, the folk tradition has not disappeared entirely (To make your own flowered eggs, see chapter 6).

On Britain's Scilly Island, forty miles (64 km) off the coast of Cornwall, the custom of egg begging has been given a distinct local character, starting with its name, egg crocking. On the Saturday before Shrove Tuesday, children beg for eggs — and if they are refused, they throw crockery.

Peculiar to three villages of Sedgemoor, England, is the tradition known as egg schackling. Each child inscribes his or her name on an egg. All of the eggs are then shaken together in a sieve until all but one are cracked. The child whose name is on the remaining egg wins a cash prize.

In Scotland, as well as in other countries, including the Netherlands, the children practice the traditional game of egg rolling. The children roll eggs down a hill; the child whose egg travels the farthest is declared the winner. Egg rolling, despite its secular sound, has symbolic meaning rooted in Christianity: The rolling egg is a metaphor for the stone that was rolled away from Christ's tomb.

The Netherlands not only shares Scotland's custom of egg rolling, but reveals further similarities to the United Kingdom with its custom of decorating "sassy" eggs — the Dutch equivalent to England's pace eggs. At Easter, a sassy egg is made by wrapping a hen's egg with flowers and leaves in a cloth, then wrapping it in another cloth with onion skin or other natural dye and boiling it for twenty minutes.

But on Palm Sunday, children in the Netherlands participate in a ritual uniquely their country's own. A symbolic palm branch known as a "palmpass" is decorated with eggshells, chocolate eggs, paper flags, oranges, and figs. Children roam with the palmpass saying: "One more Sunday and we'll get an egg, and we'll get an egg, and we'll get an egg. One egg is no egg, two eggs are half an egg, three eggs are an Easter egg." An Easter egg hunt follows on Easter Monday, at which time the children match up eggs of similar colors in preparation for egg-knocking fights.

Some cultures are noted for their chocolate eggs. In Perugia, Italy, hollow chocolate eggs are filled with surprises for the recipients. Luxembourg also is noted for its chocolate eggs. There, they are associated with romance, all within a religious context. On the middle Sunday of Lent, called Pretzel Sunday, a boy gives a girl he likes an ornately decorated cake shaped like a pretzel. If the boy's feeling is reciprocated, the girl gives him an Easter egg and promises to walk with him on Easter. Often, this egg is a hollow chocolate one filled with bonbons. In leap years, the custom is reversed. Husbands and wives, as well as unwed couples, participate in the courtship/Easter egg ritual.

Poland also uses the Easter egg in a courting ritual. Eggs are given to godparents and friends as a matter of course, but if a woman gives a man an egg, this means that she would welcome his attentions. In the past, it was common for a romantic interest to receive as many as thirty to one hundred eggs. Priests, exempt from this connotation, were free to receive eggs from everyone; their eggs were dyed red with brazilwood.

In addition to natural-dyed eggs, dyed eggs that are scratch-carved with a sharp instrument are made in Poland, as they are in most of eastern Europe. Yet another characteristic decorating technique involves intricate paper-cut designs — an indigenous Polish folk art — which are appliquéd to embellish the Polish Easter egg. Often, these appliquéd eggs take the form of a jug, with a lip and handle of cut paper; the egg itself is adorned with flowers, roosters, and other patterns that are cut from paper and applied to the eggshell.

Along with some of its neighboring countries, Poland also used to practice a dousing ritual that included the use of colored eggs. On Easter Monday, the boys practiced *dyngus* — they doused the girls with water as a symbolic wish for good looks, fertility, and health. The custom sometimes meant that the girls were dragged into nearby lakes or streams, almost like a baptism. And because it all was in good fun, and a compliment at that, the girls rewarded the boys with colored eggs.

Easter Monday in Hungary is called *Hoscolkodas,* or "dousing day." In order to make the girls good future wives, boys would pour water on them, saying: "Water for your health, water for your home, water for your land, here; water, water! Don't shriek and cry and run away; it's good for you on Dousing Day." Girls rewarded the boys with Easter eggs, as well as with hard rolls and brandy. And should anyone decide to marry on Easter, that couple was sure to receive a special Easter wedding egg.

Another purification rite hailing from pagan times that was adapted to the Christian celebration of Easter was practiced in Czechoslovakia. Like Hungary and Poland, Czechoslovakia celebrated its purification custom on Easter Monday — here, known as "the day of whipping." Boys carried beribboned willow whips to the girls "so they won't be lazy or have fleas," and at the same time, caroled for eggs.

Today's decorative eggs (above) not only are the product of household traditions but are available from retail businesses. Similarly, today's chocolate eggs (opposite) are pervasive virtually worldwide.

The traditional Greek celebration of Easter held more purely religious significance. The week prior to Lent was known as cheese week — a time of modified fasting when only cheese, eggs, and milk were eaten. The eggs consumed at the end of the week were red-dyed Easter eggs, anticipated at the onset of the fast with the recitation: "With an egg I close my mouth, with an egg I shall open it again."

In eastern Rumelia, a division of the old Ottoman Empire including Albania, Macedonia, and Thrace, at the final meal before Lent, eggs were rolled across the table in conjunction with the saying, "May Lent roll by even as this egg rolls." The last egg was strung from the ceiling for a game called *laskus,* in which participants would swing the egg with their foreheads and try to catch it in their mouths.

Belgian custom is closely akin to the American tradition of the Easter egg hunt, but with the addition of its own cultural mythology and strong Catholic influence. On Holy Thursday the church bells fall silent, according to the legend that they have flown to Rome to dine with the pope and collect the Easter eggs that they will drop, upon return, for the children to find. The bells ring again on Holy Saturday — a signal for persons to embrace their chairs, benches, or the ground, should they be outside. An Easter egg hunt follows, and a second one is held on Sunday, lest any of the eggs be overlooked.

Germany, too, observes the custom of the Easter egg hunt. In addition, it embraces the concept of an Easter Bunny, who supposedly lays red eggs on Maundy Thursday and other colors on Easter Eve. Instead of the hollow chocolate eggs filled with treats that appear in other countries, satin eggs are filled with sweets, perfumes, tiny lace handkerchiefs, and other trinkets. The eggs are used in a game in which they are struck together until broken.

Another German custom calls for decorating an egg tree, much like a Christmas tree. But instead of bibelots and assorted ornaments, the only decorations are colored eggs, which are suspended from the tree's branches. Like so many other Easter practices, the egg tree was adopted from an earlier pagan rite of spring that called for uncolored eggshells on tree branches in honor of the new season.

America's Pennsylvania Dutch brought a love for decorative eggs with them to this country. These immigrants particularly were fond of a decorating technique known as scratch carving, which was popular in the early 1800s in various parts of Europe (especially eastern Europe) and even in England. The favorite motifs of the Pennsylvania Dutch included scratch-carved tulips, hearts, birds, and scrolls. An egg typically was scratched with both the giver's and recipient's names, as well as the date. (In some instances, an egg decorated in this manner even served as a birth certificate.) The scratch carving was done with a knife, needle, or razor. The scratched-out patterns showed up white through the remaining colorfully dyed portion of the egg.

In addition to scratch-carving eggs, the Pennsylvania Dutch decorated Easter eggs with appliqué, using painted fabrics or a combination of fabric with rush pith, called binsa graws. They were not alone. Rush pith-appliquéd eggs are also a folk art of Poland and Silesia.

Other cultures utilize different appliqués in decorating eggs. In Portugal, they use seashells; in Austria, they use strips of dough. Tufts of wool and metal embellish Serbian decorative eggs.

Despite geographical distances and cultural differences, it is clear that the impulse to decorate eggs is not only universal, but serves as a way to pass on traditions and values to subsequent generations.

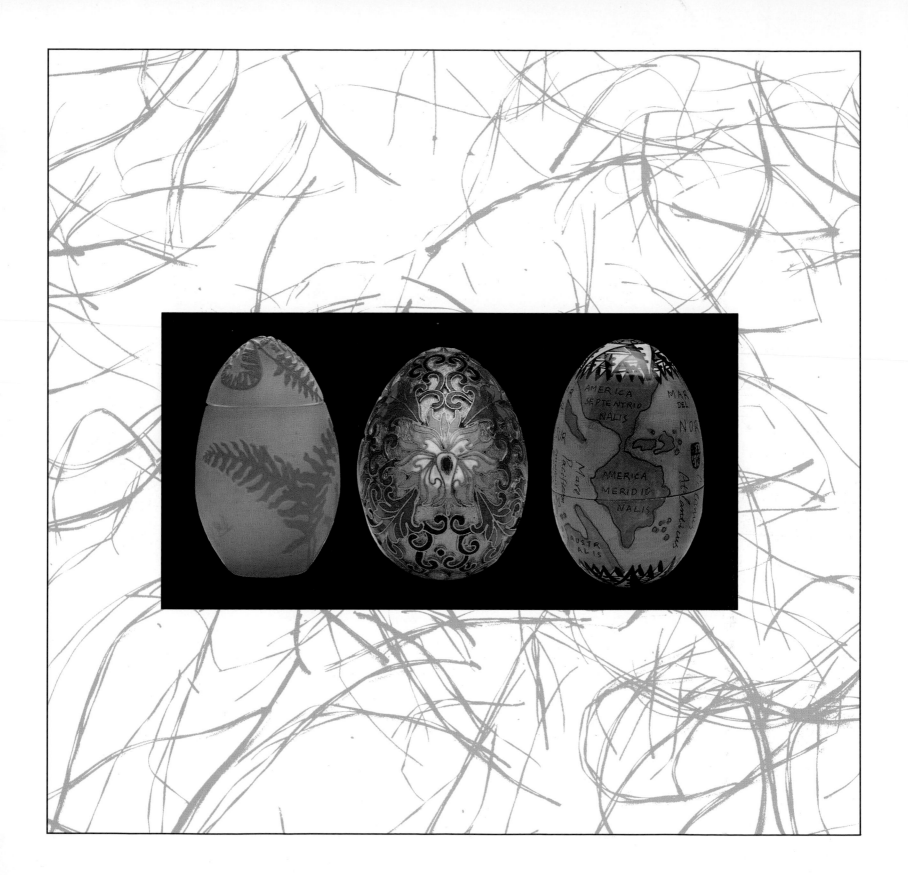

ARTIFICE AND THE EGG

While the organic hen's egg gave rise to ingenuity in decorating techniques, from ubiquitous red-dyed eggs to the flower-imprinted English pace egg, on to the complex Ukrainian wax-resist batik pysanky (see chapter 4), the concept of the decorative egg and the impulse to create it in ever-fresh variation led to yet another interpretation, one that exempted nature from the process altogether. The artificial decorative egg was inevitable: Entirely man-made, it was the next logical step from covering the natural egg with man-made ornamentation. Like the organic egg, the artificial one was subject to just as many disparate looks and cultural variations.

The oval image of the egg has been reproduced in virtually every medium known to man. It has been carved from wood, stone, and bone, and crafted in porcelain, enamel, glass, metal, and wax. By virtue of their edibility, chocolate and confectionery eggs are perhaps the artificial eggs that are closest akin to the natural egg.

Crafted in bronze, this Swedish egg, with its classic design and material, is an objet d'art.

Chocolate and Confectionery Eggs

Chocolate eggs, discussed earlier as being popular in England at the turn of the twentieth century as well as in the Netherlands and parts of Italy, have only increased in popularity with time. Fashioned from ornate molds and embellished with colored icings, left hollow, or filled with rich candy creams or fruits, nuts, caramel, or more chocolate, they are pervasive virtually worldwide. Today's chocolate eggs are not exponents of any one culture's Easter traditions, however, so much as they are an auxiliary item — a visual delight with built-in limited longevity, thanks to their primary purpose as a culinary delight.

Sugar eggs constitute a second category of consumable artificial eggs. These confectioneries often are designed as panoramics; with an oval window on one side, the interiors of these eggs contain a charming figurative scene or vignette, often including other symbols of Easter and springtime such as the hare, chicks, or ducklings. These eggs also have more of an international identity these days, popular, for instance, in Czechoslovakia as well as in the United States.

Chocolate and confectionery decorative eggs are among the most delightful to receive at Easter, as they whet the appetite as well as the eye.

Carved Eggs

Carved panoramic wooden eggs became popular in the sixteenth century after François I of France received one featuring a carving of Christ's passion. This type of artificial decorative egg became even more popular after Louis XVI presented a wooden egg to Madame Victoire, daughter of Louis XV.

In the late nineteenth century, carving eggs from boxwood was a common hobby in England. Unlike the French panoramic wooden eggs, carved boxwood eggs did not depict scenes but were carved with simple curvilinear motifs — horizontal bands of circles bisected by vertical rows of honeycomb holes. During this period, prisoners and sailors carved boxwood pomanders, egg-shaped containers that unscrewed in the middle and were used as receptacles for potpourri.

Homogeneous only in that they are made by a similar technique, carved eggs from different countries reflect cultural diversity: The Japanese ivory-carved egg with fish motifs (left) is distinctly different from wooden eggs from Switzerland (opposite, bottom) and from Hungary (opposite, top).

Bone eggs, although rarer than boxwood eggs, were carved according to the same general design patterns, which suggests that they probably were crafted at about the same time. Ivory also was used for carving eggs, some of which were hinged to provide storage for sewing threads and thimbles.

In eastern Europe, wooden eggs were especially popular for children because of their resistance to breakage. For the most part, these eggs were made of plain, unadorned wood. Only in the Ukraine were they a true folk-art form, inlaid with mother-of-pearl.

Smooth-surfaced eggs carved from onyx are popular today in Mexico. Bearing no ornamental surface carving, they gain charm through the striations of the stone itself, the glossy polished surface, and the egg's substantial physical weight. More valuable eggs also are carved from semiprecious stones such as malachite and lapis.

Virtually every substance suitable for carving has been enlisted to fashion decorative eggs—even petrified palm tree (below). The carved egg (right) hails from the United States.

In Australia, eggs from indigenous birds such as the ostrich and the emu are decoratively carved. Shown here are hand-carved Australian emu eggs.

*O*ne of the most remarkable aesthetic
features of decorative eggs is their tactile
appeal. Textural traits vary with cultures,
from the ivory-carved Japanese egg and
wood-carved Romanian eggs covered with
beads to the Californian chicken egg
wrapped in ovoid pheasant feathers.

Painted Porcelain Eggs

For centuries, porcelain eggs have been a decorative arts mainstay. One of the most prolific producers of these artificial eggs were the Russians. The nineteenth century marked the zenith of their porcelain Easter egg craft.

Russian eggs were icons of sorts, and were beautifully decorated with resurrection scenes. Typically, they were hollow with a hole at each end for ornamentation. While royalty received the most elaborately painted eggs, many plainer ones were made at the Russian Imperial porcelain factory for members of the royal family to bestow as tokens of appreciation to friends and staff. These particular eggs bore the royal monogram of the bestower in gold as well as less ornate designs, such as an inscription reading "Christos Voskres" ("Christ is risen").

Porcelain eggs inevitably served as documentation of their heyday's history. In Russia during World War I, for instance, a red cross was emblazoned on an otherwise all-white porcelain egg. In early nineteenth-century Germany, which borrowed the idea of porcelain eggs from Russia, porcelain eggs were adorned with scenes of soldiers in eighteenth-century uniform. Later in the century, such eggs commemorated historical events such as the German acquisition of Alsace in 1871.

In addition to fine porcelain eggs (which continue to be popular in many countries, and are crafted not only by china manufacturers but individual craftspersons as well), artificial eggs crafted from clay include other less white varieties. Among the best known of these folk-art eggs are the faience eggs of

Delicately painted in keeping with its fragile medium, this porcelain egg was made in Hungary.

Eggs made from clay are crafted from Europe to the Orient. The two porcelain eggs (top, left to right) are from France and England; the Japanese glazed pottery egg dates back to 1900.

When painted and displayed on individual stands, common goose eggs become arresting collectibles.

the Kutahya potters in northwest Asia Minor. White with distinctive blue-green glazes for patterns, the eggs featured simple folk designs such as angels, on to more intricate florals and swags. Although the pottery was long run primarily by Armenians, the faience style was Islamic because the eggs were marketed mainly to Turkish Muslims.

Today, contemporary potters continue to explore the decorative egg as a creative form. Glazes render beautiful rainbow colors typically associated with dyed Easter eggs, while the textural interest they produce is unique to the medium. One potter I know of specializes in clay eggs of varying sizes and glazes; each one, he contends, is imbued with the mystical, magical qualities inherent in the form and all that it symbolizes.

The Russian tradition of decorating eggs continues today, as exemplified by hand-painted eggs celebrating Christianity.

Battersea Enamel Eggs

Nutmeg was an important spice in England in the middle of the eighteenth century and was used to enhance wine, ale, and foods. At this time, nutmeg graters frequently were made in the shape of an egg out of Battersea enamel. Battersea enamel eggs were popular again in the early 1800s and put to practical use as snuffboxes.

Glass Eggs

Glass eggs, among the most beautiful and fragile of all decorative eggs, historically associated Easter with courtship rituals. Both German and Alsatian glassblowers created elaborate eggs to impress their girlfriends. An Alsatian egg made in Solbach and dated 1765, for example, was inscribed with: "With all my love and all my faith this Easter egg I give to you."

Contemporary glassblowers seldom consider courtship when crafting their eggs; instead, each is a work of art intended for admiration. But even these contemporary eggs, though, sometimes serve to reveal the historical context in which they were crafted: When the United States' Mount Saint Helens volcano erupted, its ash was used by glassblowers to fashion beautifully striated eggs, among other objets d'art.

Glass eggs possess an inherent, simple beauty. The egg shown here was crafted in France.

Elegant accessory items for the home, glass eggs lend themselves to creative displays.

Wax

All-wax eggs derived from Russia, the first probably from the Candle Works of the Orthodox church. Nuns made the eggs and decorated them for Easter with tiny colored beads embedded in the wax in different designs, crosses, and flowers, most commonly. As the influence of the Orthodox church spread beyond Russia, so did the popularity of the wax egg. It was brought to Israel, and then to England. Arab Orthodox sisters in both Jerusalem and England continue to produce the eggs. Ribbons are attached to one end of the eggs so they can be hung alongside the family icons.

Metal Eggs

Decorative eggs worked from precious metals reached a pinnacle of style and opulence with those by Fabergé for the Imperial Russian family (see chapter 5) in the late nineteenth century. Since then, many eggs made from metal have attempted to emulate the Fabergé prototype and paradigm of style. For example, contemporary Texas jeweler Robert Whiteside uses lavish amounts of precious metals and gems in the guilloche enamel art objects he unabashedly bases on the Fabergé style (see chapter 5, page 82). His eggs include a guilloche-latticed presentation egg in red enamel that is mounted on a crystal base; a lilac enamel guilloche clock egg studded with pearls, amethysts, and diamonds, and simpler varieties such as a royal blue enamel egg swagged with guilloche and mounted on a fluted column plinth.

Heavily detailed, this Austro-Hungarian metal egg exudes a flamboyance that rivals that of Russian eggs.

Popular in the East, cloisonné, an enamel decoration over metal, has been used to create a rich repository of decorative eggs.

On these Chinese cloisonné eggs, enamel was applied and fired on brass over clay.

Metal eggs constitute what are probably the most formal and ornate of all decorative eggs. Shown here are (above) a box of ten Taiwanese cloisonné eggs; (right) a silver egg from Russia; and (opposite) a French egg standing on cabriole legs.

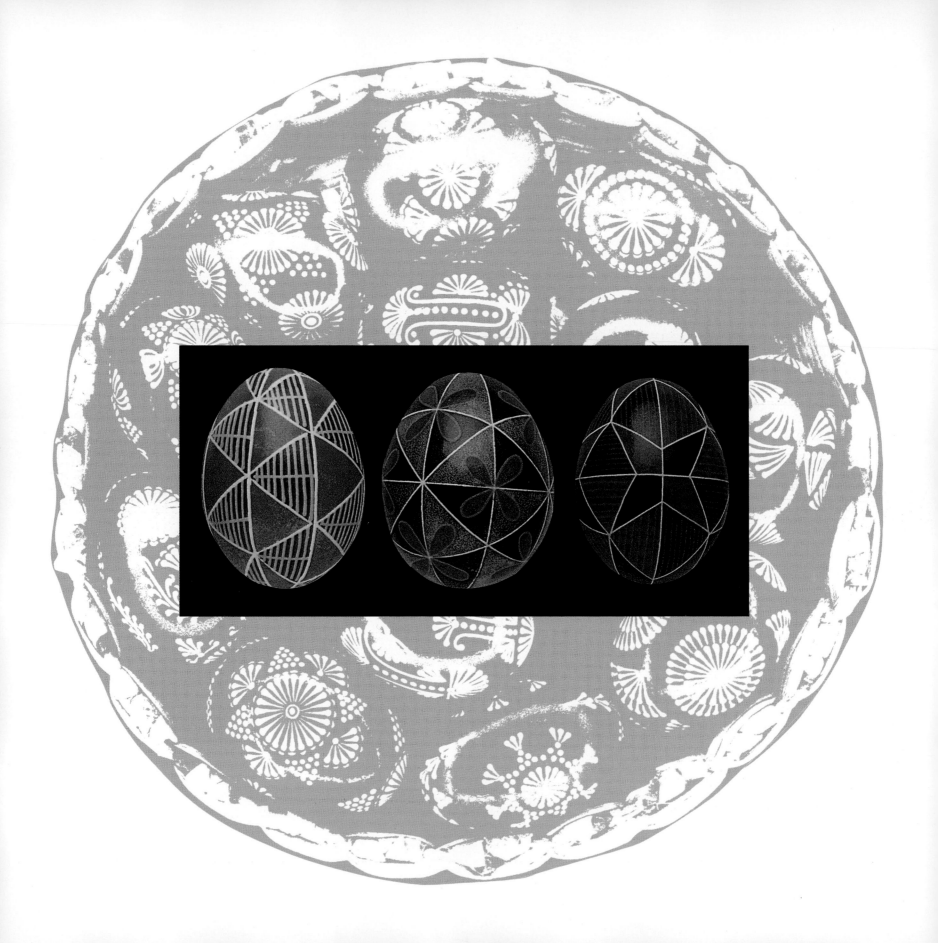

Eggs in Eastern Europe

Ukrainian Prototypes

As a symbol of fertility, the egg naturally was held in high esteem by one of the world's most fertile regions — Europe's breadbasket, the Ukraine. The egg played a stellar role in the spring rites of Ukrainian primeval man as the perfect emblem of life's continuity and propagation: The embryo incubating in the eggshell before hatching new life served as an ideal metaphor for winter's dormancy before spring's rebirth — too much so to go unheeded.

Not one artist or cluster of artists, but the entire Ukrainian culture, developed and practiced the wax-resist batik method of egg decorating known as *pysanky,* which means "to write." These brilliantly colored eggs were symbolic, not only in the generic sense of the egg, but in every specific detail as well. Each color of dye had a different meaning, as did each design motif. For the pagan culture, exchanging pysanky was a gesture of peace and goodwill, the message tailored by the giver to address the specific needs of the recipient (that is, food if the recipient had a poor harvest, good health if he or she is or had been ill, and so on). Whereas teens might receive pysanky with a white background, representing the unlimited potential of a pure and unblemished

Since pagan times, eastern European countries have decorated eggs to bring luck and ward off evil.

future, like a tabula rasa, the elderly might receive black eggs patterned with motifs such as ladders and gates, which suggest the journey after death.

Because the Ukraine spans a large geographic area, there are noticeable regional distinctions. The pysanky of the Hutsuls in the Carpathian Mountains are complex geometrical patterns, while the pysanky made across the steppes to the east are more florid and baroque.

While no two pysanky are exactly alike, there is some uniformity in the symbolic meaning of colors and designs — a code that continues even today.

White, as mentioned, represents purity, while black suggests the darkest period before dawn. Yellow symbolizes both a prosperous harvest and wisdom; green, rebirth and all its connotations — freshness, innocence, and youth. Orange is an important color because, as it is a combination of the yellow of wisdom and the red of passion, it creates the color of the sun as well as its warmth, attendant power, and endurance. Brown evokes the earth itself and expresses a positive connectedness with it. Purple, although usually associated with royalty, represents faith and trust on pysanky. A combination of black and white together is a summons for protection from harm and often is used on those eggs made to honor the dead.

Simple floral motifs represent love and charity; wavy lines symbolize eternity: Both transform eggs into folk art.

Among Ukrainian pysanky, eggs decorated with a wax-resist batik technique, each design motif has its own meaning, as do each of the animals decorating this collection.

Any Ukrainian receiving a pysanky emblazoned with a motif of the sun would know that good fortune was smiled upon him or her by the person bestowing the egg. Similarly, patterns of storks, chickens, or roosters represent the fulfillment of wishes, specifically for fertility. Deer, horses, and rams are emblems for prosperity and wealth, and an endless wavy line symbolizes eternity. Love and charity are communicated on pysanky by a floral design, eternal youth by a fir tree (or any evergreen). Wolves' teeth indicate protection, and the lion, strength. Triangles, common on pysanky, stand for any trio: the elements of fire, wind, and water; mother, father, and child; or, after Christianity, the Holy Trinity. Cross-hatching and dots do not expressly have meaning but are used as design filler for border patterns. One of the most powerful symbols decorating pysanky is the circle. With no beginning and no end, the circle is regarded as impenetrable by evil, making it a potent symbol of protection. After the introduction of Christianity, pysanky often featured Christian symbols — fish, crosses, and crowns of thorns.

Pysanky Lore and Legend

Like other folk arts, pysanky is surrounded by its own share of lore and legend. One poignant legend of pysanky's origins holds that migrating birds, during one particularly bitter winter, were frozen midair, falling to the ground. Peasants rescued the dying creatures and warmed them in their huts. The birds recovered and, when freed at springtime, returned to the peasants bearing pysanky as tokens of their gratitude.

Almost all of the early legends surrounding pysanky point to the Ukrainians' love of and respect for nature. For the pre-Christian peasant, nature was the capricious judge whose verdict could go either in favor of or against the succession of life. In pagan times, then, pysanky were created only in the springtime and were used in rites of worship to the sun. The egg yolk was considered a microcosm of the sun, a purveyor of life to be respected. Physically reminiscent of the sun, the yolk represented the victory of life over death; of the return of the bountiful spring sun after winter's killing bleakness.

On Ukrainian eggs, wavy lines represent eternity, while circles, having neither beginning nor end through which evil can penetrate, are intended to offer protection from harm.

Eggs were used in more than one way among the various sectors of pagan Ukrainians. Convinced of decorative eggs' powers, farmers rubbed them across the chests of oxen and other work animals to ensure that their harnesses would not painfully rub against them and reduce their efficiency. After thus providing for the well-being of their beasts, the farmers then buried the eggs in the earth to solicit similar aid and protection for their crops. In addition, eggs were strung along the barn door to guard against the danger of fire.

Already rich with symbolism and an entrenched part of Ukrainian life, pysanky were readily adapted from rituals of spring to rituals of Easter after the introduction of Christianity.

In Christian times, the creation of pysanky fell within the domain of women, who approached the art with a sense of reverence and preparedness. It was important that the woman's spirit be as pure as possible before beginning the decorating process. To that end, the day before decorating began was spent quietly with family, avoiding friends and the temptation to engage in idle chatter. Decorating began the next evening, after the children were put to bed and assurances made that no males in the household were observing. Only those females of the same household decorated together, as no one wanted to risk having their ideas copied. The eggs were kept hidden until their debut in church on Easter Sunday.

Each egg required a different blessing for the conveyance of different wishes, but the overall purpose behind decorating was to imbue the egg with the goodness of the household and thereby ward off evil. Special songs were quietly sung as the pysanky were prepared. The fresh eggs used for decorating were collected only from hens within the proximity of a rooster, for the use of an infertile egg would suggest infertility of the household itself.

*Traditionally made by the women in a family, eastern European eggs
(opposite) often were ornamented with the designs of the decorator's favorite
flowers. In all early cultures, including that of the Ukraine, red eggs (above)
were believed to be imbued with special magical powers.*

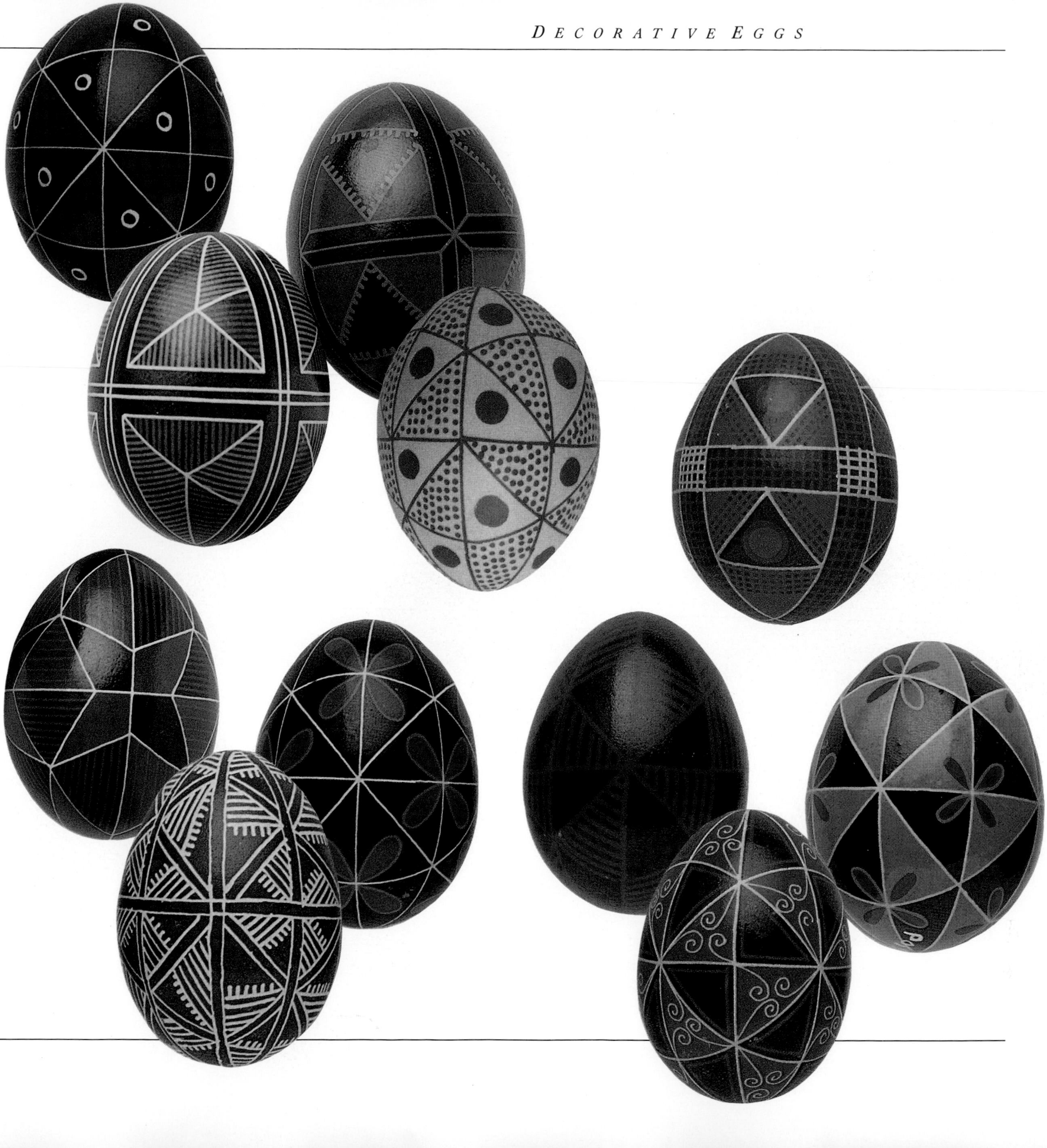

Over a period of several days, great care was spent decorating. (Obviously, the amount of time required to make each egg varied, but today a complex egg design takes about three hours.) Pysanky eggs were not boiled or blown, but were decorated with their contents intact. (Over a period of time, the contents turn to powder.) Dyes were made from natural materials and were contained in small clay pots. For a yellow dye, wild apple bark, buckwheat husks, campion, lilac, or dog fennel flower was used. Red dye was extracted from cochineal, deer horn, and sandalwood, and a darker red from black hollyhock, bush anemones, birch leaves, and moss. Green was made from sunflower seeds and wild elderberries; black, from the young leaves of the black maple and dark periwinkle; dark yellow, from alder buds, hazel and chestnut leaves, and walnut, apple, or oak bark.

The pysanky technique of drawing involves dividing the egg into equal segments with vertical and horizontal lines—an approach clearly evident in this collection of the "Forty Triangles" motif. An important symbol, the triangle can refer to any trinity—water, earth, and fire; Father, Son, and Holy Spirit.

Using an instrument called a stylus, the decorators drew on the desired design with wax. Balance was achieved by the careful placement of color and motif, as well as proportion. (See chapter 6 for instructions on how to make pysanky.) By Maundy Thursday, the decorating was complete, with as many as sixty eggs having been decorated by a single, large family.

At the same time Ukrainian women were making pysanky they also were preparing the solid-colored dyed eggs known as *krashanky,* which means "color." Unlike pysanky, krashanky are boiled before they are dyed and are intended to be eaten after they are used in children's games. In fact, they are the first foods to be consumed after the long Lenten fast.

To understand the significance of decorative eggs in the Ukrainian culture, it is important to look at the seriousness with which the Ukrainians regarded Easter. This was no casual holiday or single day of sober religious experience. Beginning with Ash Wednesday, a full forty days were invested, preparing body, mind, soul, and home for Easter day.

During the Lenten season, the home was thoroughly cleaned; mattresses were aired, the keeping room was whitewashed, rugs were beaten — every square inch of home was scrubbed to a fine shine and thus made pure for Easter. The body also was cleansed and readied. A rigorous forty-day fast required abstention from meat, eggs, and dairy products on Mondays, Wednesdays, and Fridays. The fast was approached with seriousness; each family and each individual willingly and lovingly sacrificed an important part of their diet to purge impurities in anticipation of the upcoming holy day. In addition, at least one new item of clothing was made for Easter due to an ancient custom from pagan times in which peasants bedecked themselves in fresh attire to complement the freshness and beauty of spring.

The last week of Lent was church oriented. On Maundy Thursday (called *Strastney Chetver*), the priest read twelve different sections of the Bible that described the suffering of Christ. Between each interval, the congregation touched their heads to the floor three times, rendering older churches' floors wavily warped from repetition of the ritual. On Good Friday, believers gathered in church again, this time around a large painting of the crucified Christ that was at the front of the church, by the altar. Candles were lit and church lamps were dimmed, setting an appropriately somber mood for the mourning of Christ's tomb.

During the last few days of Lent, special Easter foods were prepared: "paska" (an Easter bread), hams and sausages, and a bitter concoction of horseradish, beets, vinegar, and honey that was intended to make its partakers mindful of the bitter sufferings Christ endured.

Easter Eve was celebrated by a midnight mass that lasted more than two hours. At midnight, the priest proclaimed, "Khrystos Voskres" ("Christ is risen"), and the congregation answered, "Voisteno Voskres" ("He is risen, indeed"). To this mass, each family brought a carefully packed picnic basket for the priest to sprinkle with holy water and bless at the end of the service. The basket, lined with a beautifully embroidered cloth and topped with another, contained the paska, horseradish mixture, and, among other things, a few dyed krashanky and decorated pysanky.

No wonder, given the Ukrainians' total commitment to observing Lent, that decorative eggs, too, were regarded so seriously.

Easter Sunday was the culmination of the events of the past forty days. Finally, eggs were exchanged, again, with the greeting, "Khrystos Voskres," and the response, "Voisteno Voskres."

The officially blessed Easter basket contents were eaten, and families took time to honor their dead by moving the Easter day celebration to the cemeteries, where the children played games with krashanky. Other krashanky were broken and the hard-boiled eggs, as well as their shells, were sprinkled over the graves. According to Ukrainian legend, the birds that later came to eat the eggs actually were the souls of the deceased loved ones who had been honored. In addition to scattering broken krashanky over the graves, the Ukrainian people took at least three or four pysanky to the cemetery to leave at the grave sites.

Finally, the pysanky made by a single family might have been distributed as follows: a couple of eggs presented to the priest; ten to fifteen given to young children; another ten to fifteen exchanged between the unwed young men and women; several saved to protect the aging who might face death during the upcoming year; others retained to guard the home and barn from havoc by the elements; and several used in the age-old custom of ensuring fertility of the field and farm as well as a bountiful harvest.

Today, the tradition of creating pysanky continues, even among Ukrainian immigrants to other countries. Examples of the work are on exhibit at Ukrainian museums in both New York City and Chicago and elsewhere in the world. In addition, as a beautifully decorative folk art, pysanky has been taken up by contemporary craftspersons and artists outside the Ukrainian ethnic background. Pysanky's growth in visibility and popularity beyond its culture of origin in no way lessens its importance to the Ukrainian people, however. In fact, Ukrainians are expanding the genre, now making wooden pysanky that capture the beauty and traditional symbolism of the traditional eggshell pysanky, but without the real egg's fragility.

The advent of Christianity in the Ukraine resulted in yet more symbols as pysanky motifs—those of a religious nature, as seen in this sampling (opposite).

The Lithuanian Legacy

Like the Ukraine, nearby Lithuania had an abiding regard for decorative eggs at Easter, and Lithuanians created both scratch-pattern and wax-resist varieties. After a purification of home and heart, much like that observed in the Ukraine, Lithuanians turned their attention to eggs for the first time on Palm Sunday. The first person out of bed that morning grabbed a willow branch and began playfully lashing at those still sleeping, as he or she demanded an egg for Easter. This custom was practiced by children, who playfully struck their parents, and also by young, unmarried men, who would strike their potential future wives in a kind of courtship ritual.

More so than in the Ukraine, scratch-carved eggs were among the most prevalent of Lithuanian decorative eggs. These eggs were dyed in baths made of natural materials, and were passed from one color bath to another for more unusual color variation. The eggs were allowed to dry, then were ornamented with motifs scratched from the dyed egg with a sharp knife or piece of glass. Most of the designs involved short lines, zigzags, or imprecise curves, as straight lines are much easier to carve than curvilinear forms. Some of the patterns are quite primitive in appearance and are believed to be the oldest Lithuanian eggs. A striking resemblance exists between these primitive motifs and those found on Lithuanian bronzes and silvers from the eleventh to fifteenth centuries, leading to the theory that similar scratch designs on eggs were conceived at the same time.

Unlike the Ukrainian egg decorators, who were the matrons, the decorators of scratch-carved eggs in Lithuania were youths who had been tutored by the older generation. The passing on of technique and design from one generation

A collection of Lithuanian eggs by Jouzas Jasiunas (opposite) was made with the wax-resist method, which utilizes a straight pin tool for drawing designs in wax.

to the next ensured continuity of a major folk art. This transfer of the torch was critical: Lithuanian Easter eggs were not preserved from one year to the next, making hands-on lessons and awareness of the process imperative if the chain of history was to go unbroken.

Virtually every country in eastern Europe has produced some form of decorative egg akin to the Ukraine's wax-resist pysanky. Lithuanian batik eggs have a look that is their own, however, not only as a result of different Easter traditions (and thus different decorative symbols), but also because of the use of different tools. The Ukrainians make pysanky using a hollow stylus for applying the heated wax, while Lithuanians use a delicate nail, drawing pin, fish bone, or wooden splinter. Not only do Lithuanian eggs feature symbols different from those on pysanky, but the meaning of the Lithuanian symbols has been lost over time, whereas the Ukrainians have retained knowledge of their symbols' meanings.

What is amazing about Lithuanian Easter eggs is not the fact that the designs have resisted deciphering and comprehending after their meanings were lost over time, but that thousands of design variations were passed on from older to younger generations through visual memory. Lithuanian eggs were not saved from year to year. And with no benefit of photography and no extant examples of egg designs to emulate, the traditional patterns and techniques required keen attention in order to be remembered at Easter each year. Passed on in this way, the designs understandably might be limited to a handful of motifs, but this is not the case. The great depth of the design pool can be explained, in part, by competition: Each family wanted its eggs to be more creatively patterned and colored than its neighbor's.

Lithuanian scratch-carved eggs by Maria Gotceitas (opposite, left) and Lithuanian wax-resist eggs by Linda Markut (opposite, right) represent the continuation of their culture's ancient tradition.

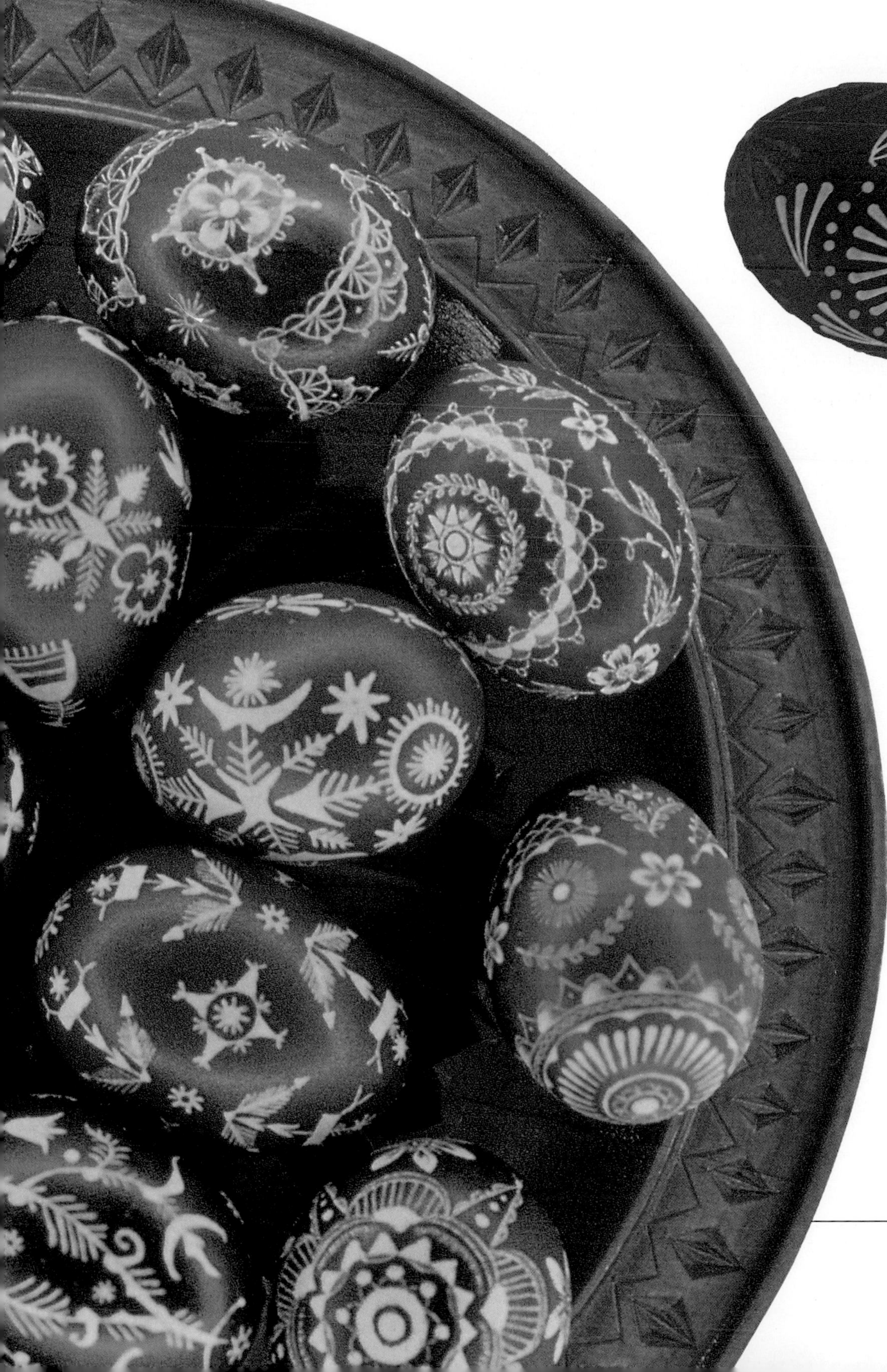

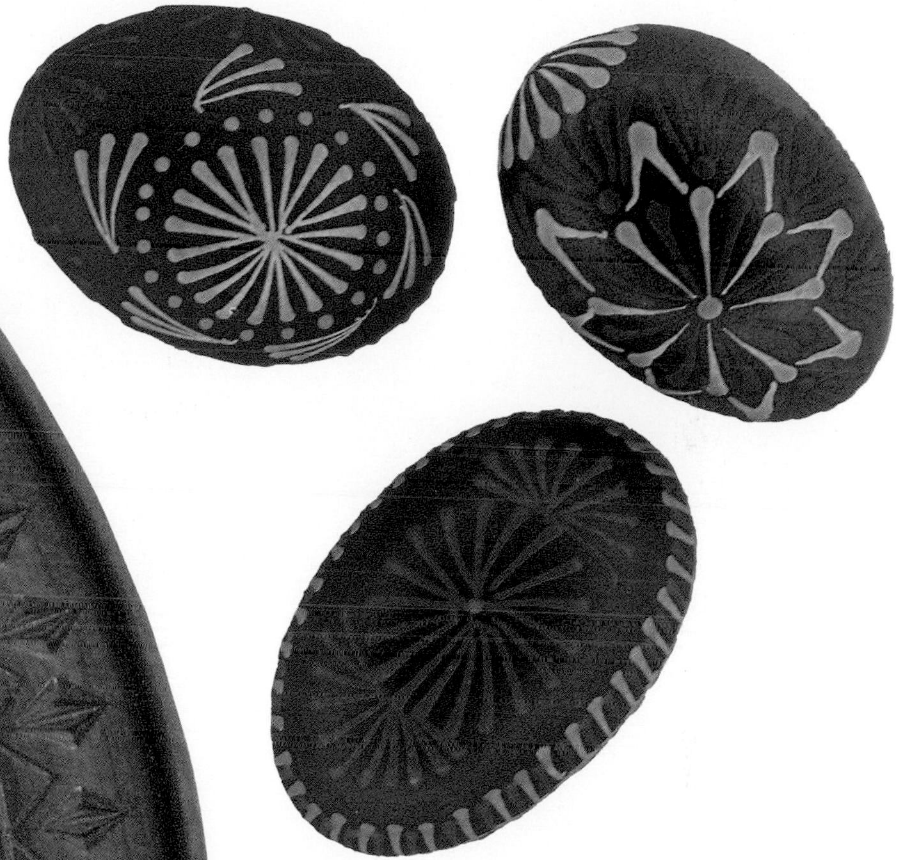

CHAPTER FIVE

FABERGÉ'S FLIGHTS OF FANTASY

Into the Public Eye

Of all the artificial decorative eggs ever made, those crafted for the Imperial family of prerevolutionary Russia by the shop of the artist-jeweler Peter Carl Fabergé are exemplary. Crafted from gold, silver, enamel, jewels, pearls, and semiprecious stones, the Fabergé Easter eggs constitute an archetype emulated even today. Thanks to the efforts of the late Armand Hammer, an American physician who spent nine years in Russia (from 1921 to 1930) with the intent of opening a field hospital to combat the raging typhus epidemic there, these eggs were not lost in the annals of history, languishing unheeded by the international eye.

Upon his visit to Russia, Hammer discovered an even more serious peril than typhus: famine. To help alleviate that situation, he arranged the first barter agreement with Russia, which exchanged Soviet commodities, including furs and hides, for American wheat. During the nine years he spent in the country, Hammer amassed a truly incredible collection of art, including fifteen of

This elaborate cloisonné Fabergé egg (above) was made in the earlier part of this century. The Spring Flower Egg (opposite) was created in 1890.

Fabergé's exquisite eggs, which he obtained through the Ministry of Foreign Trade. Upon return to the states, Hammer opened Hammer Galleries in Manhattan. The eggs that formed a portion of his inventory won immediate attention from the public and the press; this attention was repeated with each sale, as Hammer divested himself of the Romanov treasures.

Head of the House

Peter Carl Fabergé, though best remembered for the opulence of his designs, really was operating from a much different mind-set. Extravagance for its own sake — that is, pricey materials crafted for showy effect — was not his intent.

In 1914, at the age of sixty-eight, he explained:

> Clearly, if you compare my things with those of such firms as Tiffany, Boucheron and Cartier, of course you will find that the value of theirs is greater than of mine. As far as they are concerned, it is possible to find a necklace in stock for one and a half million roubles. But of course these people are merchants and not artist-jewellers. Expensive things interest me little if the value is merely in so many diamonds or pearls.

The value of his work, as Fabergé saw it, was in the design — its creativity, cleverness (as a rule, his Imperial eggs contained hidden surprises, such as miniature portraits in jewel frames, golden hens, miniature royal coaches), and meticulous execution. If precious materials were compatible with, and enhanced, the design, and if the object's recipient was of a station in life that behooved the use of such materials, certainly Fabergé was not opposed to their utilization.

Fabergé was nothing short of a genius: He was an artist, a craftsman, and an inspiration for those who worked in his shop. The standards he set were so high, so crystalline, and immutable by definition that the outpouring of designs from the House of Fabergé, though executed by many different artisans, bore amazing consistency in both quality and style.

Fabergé rose to his calling as an artist-jeweler in 1870 at the young age of twenty-four. At that time, he took over as head of the small, rather unexceptional jewelry business started by his father, Gustav, in the Russian Imperial capital, St. Petersburg. A French Protestant by ancestry, Peter Carl Fabergé was educated in Germany. He learned the family business through apprenticeships with several of Europe's prominent goldsmiths. He was also cognizant of what had gone before him in the medium, having visited major royal and state collections in Italy, England, France, and Germany. Although he was young when he assumed responsibility for the family business, Fabergé was no neophyte; he was educated in technique and possessed a cultivated eye.

His role, as Fabergé saw it, was not to physically work on any of the pieces that bore his shop's name, but, rather, to supervise and ensure state-of-the-art quality and unprecedented creativity. Indeed, the term "Fabergé eggs" is a bit misleading: None of the eggs were made by Fabergé himself. Instead, they were designed and crafted by extraordinarily talented jewelers whom Fabergé managed to attract and retain. Fabergé divided his shop into areas of specialization, with separate divisions for conventional jewelry, dinner silver, stone carvings, old-style Russian works, and more contemporary enamel arts. His ability to cultivate and motivate artisans in so many areas of the field is

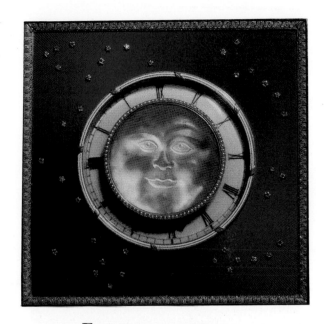

Fabergé's Man in the Moon Clock can be seen in the Forbes Magazine Collection, New York, New York.

Popular as commemorative gifts, Fabergé's miniature eggs measured less than an inch (2.5 cm) high.

responsible for the House of Fabergé's uncontested reputation not only during Fabergé's lifetime, but even today. Fabergé created much more than fine objets d'art and art jewelry: He created fantasies.

One of the two jewelers most intimately involved with the near-mythical Fabergé eggs was Michael Evlampievich Perchin. Like Fabergé himself, Perchin's talent manifested early. At the age of twenty-six, in 1886, Perchin became the leading work master for the house. All of the signed Imperial Easter eggs predating 1903 bear his initials. Perchin was distinguished from his colleagues not only by his ability, but by being one of the few native Russians employed in the predominantly Scandinavian shop.

The second jeweler due major credit for the renowned Fabergé eggs is Henrik Wigstrom. Wigstrom, two years younger even than Perchin, was a Swedish Finn who apprenticed under Perchin until he finally succeeded him. After 1903, all of the signed Imperial eggs feature Wigstrom's mark. This does not mean, however, that no other metal smiths contributed to the awe-inspiring creations: Only approximately half of the eggs bear a maker's signature stamp.

In addition to the artisan's stamp, Fabergé eggs feature two other identifying marks. One indicates the purity of the metal content, and the other represents the city of origin. For St. Petersburg, the symbol was a pair of crossed anchors; for Moscow, St. George and the dragon. A national mark began to replace the regional stamps after 1896. The national symbol was a profile of a woman in the traditional Russian headdress known as *kokoshnik*.

Elevating the Egg

The first Russian Imperial egg is believed to have been made in 1886, although the exact date and circumstances of its execution are a subject of debate. It is known that this particular egg was presented by Czar Alexander III to his wife, Maria, a few years after the assassination of his father, Alexander II. One theory holds that Alexander III commissioned Fabergé to create an Easter surprise of beauty and imagination for his wife to help her over the melancholy and anxiety she suffered as a result of her father-in-law's death. Another school suggests that the czar never commissioned the egg at all, but that Fabergé, hoping to win Alexander III's royal patronage, took it upon himself to create and present the Easter surprise. The conclusion that 1886 was the year that the egg was made is based largely on the fact that it was the year in which Perchin became Fabergé's work master. Whatever the specifics of its origins, that first Easter egg marked the beginning of a tradition that continued through 1916 and, in all, produced some fifty-three eggs.

By the time Czar Alexander III's throne was passed on to his son, Nicholas II, in 1894, the custom of the czar presenting a Fabergé surprise Easter egg to the czarina was firmly established. Nicholas II, incompetent in many ways, at least proved an able torchbearer in this area, as he not only perpetuated the egg-giving custom but enlarged its scope with presentations not only to his wife, Alexandra Feodorovna, but also to his mother, Maria.

Subdued compared to later eggs, the first Imperial egg (left) is believed to have been made in 1886. The Austrian Surprise Egg (right) illustrates Fabergé's delight in hidden components.

The first Imperial egg appears extremely simple when compared to later eggs. Only two and one-half inches (6.25 cm) in height, it is made entirely of gold, with its outside enameled a matte white to convincingly appear as an eggshell. The egg opens, wherein lies the surprise: a plump golden hen with ruby eyes, nesting on golden straw in the gold interior of the eggshell.

By 1898, when Alexander Ferdinandovich Kelch presented one of goldsmith Michael Perchin's Fabergé eggs to his wife, Siberian mining heiress Barbara Bazanov, the style of fantasy eggs had evolved into one of greater exuberance. Based on the same concept as the original Imperial egg, the Kelch Hen Egg, as this non-Imperial egg is called, looks little like its antecedent. Whereas the first Imperial egg sought to resemble an actual eggshell, the Kelch Hen Egg was boldly enameled a brilliant red over the fine texturing of a guilloche gold ground. (Guilloche appears frequently on Fabergé eggs. It is a surface of enamel that has been engraved by hand or by engine. As many as five or six separate layers of enamel, all individually baked, make up a guilloche.) The Kelch Hen Egg's vertical center was circumscribed in diamonds, and the egg placed atop an almost four-inch (10-cm) gold stand swagged with gold petals inset with diamonds (the stand, however, was a later addition, not a part of the original presentation piece).

The creative genius behind this egg is found in certain ironies: Opening the regally decorated exterior lengthwise, one finds a diametric contrast — a white interior, which resembles the glossy white of a boiled egg fresh out of the shell, in the center of which is a realistic yellow enamel yolk. The yolk opens to reveal a gold hen enameled in natural shades of rust, copper, and brown. Within the hen awaits yet another surprise: a gold folding easel, only one and seven-eighths inches (4.7 cm) tall, that holds a rose diamond frame and portrait of Barbara

Modeled after the first Imperial egg, Fabergé's Kelch Hen Egg (opposite), 1898, features red enamel over a guilloche gold ground.

Bazanov Kelch. (The original portrait has since been replaced with a miniature painting of Czarevich Alexis cloaked in the Imperial family's Fourth Rifle Battalion of Guards' uniform.)

But the House of Fabergé didn't limit itself to variations on the theme of a hen in an egg in its elaborate fantasy Easter eggs. The most famous of the Imperial Easter eggs is the Coronation Egg. A true masterpiece, this egg was signed by Perchin for presentation in 1897 by Czar Nicholas II to his wife, Alexandra Feodorovna. The labor-intensive egg is covered with starburst patterns, created by detailed engraving of gold, which are enameled a shimmering topaz. Atop the starbursts rest gold trellises of laurel, which extend over the entire egg; black enamel Imperial eagles with diamond centers are mounted at each point of tangency on the laurel trellises. Both ends of the egg are encrusted with table diamonds and other jewels set into engraved gold mounts.

Inside, the egg contains a richly detailed, exact miniature replica of the coronation coach. Although the egg bears Perchin's mark, the coach itself was crafted over a fifteen-month period under Perchin's supervision by George Stein. A former coachman turned goldsmith, Stein was perfect for the job. The details of the carriage are exquisite: The actual coronation coach's red lacquer and velvet upholstery are reproduced in rich red enamel; chased gold replicates the real vehicle's gilt wood frame. The large coach's iron wheels are copied in platinum, and its glass windows in etched rock crystals, on the miniature. Topping the carriage is an Imperial crown of rose diamonds and, inside, are light blue enamel curtains and a turquoise enamel ceiling. Originally, a tiny gold egg hung from a hook inside the carriage, but it has been lost over the years.

Just as each individual egg exemplifies unbridled imagination in the nature of the hidden surprise and how it relates to the whole, so does the repertoire of eggs when considered collectively. There was no dearth of diversity in the multitudinous designs created by the House of Fabergé. Easter eggs not only featured the traditional symbols of the season, such as hens and eggs, but more generic allusions, as well. In Russia, spring's first flowers spawned inordinate joy and celebration after the bleakness of the long winter.

The Fabergé artists captured this cultural sentiment toward the season in the Spring Flower Egg, made in 1890 for Czar Alexander III's presentation to Czarina Maria Feodorovna. Signed by Michael Perchin, the ornately engraved, red-enamel-over-gold egg is suspended in a rococo gold cage encrusted with diamonds. The egg's gold pedestal is set in a fluted bowenite (pale jade) base banded with rose diamonds. Opened lengthwise from the top, the egg proffers a jubilant ode to spring: a resplendent basket of spring wood anemones. Each flower has petals of white chalcedony with garnet centers, engraved gold stems, and green enamel leaves. The basket itself is Gothic in design and is worked in platinum studded with rose diamonds.

Also a celebration of life, one of the most detailed eggs takes the form of a miniature topiary orange tree. Made in 1911 for Nicholas II to present to his mother, the Orange Tree Egg exemplifies the trend toward larger scale that characterizes the Imperial eggs. It spans ten and one-half inches (26.25 cm) closed, nearly twelve inches (30 cm) open, as compared to the first Imperial egg, which was only two and one-half inches (6.25 cm) long.

The Orange Tree Egg is also a testament to the increasing opulence of the royal Easter eggs. Sprouting delicately carved dark green nephrite (a variety of jade) leaves from gold branches, the tree issues forth minuscule white enamel blossoms with diamond centers, which are juxtaposed with oranges of citrine, amethyst, champagne diamonds, and subtly colored sapphire. The golden trunk

Pages 86-87:

The most famous of the Imperial Easter eggs is the Coronation Egg (left), made by Fabergé's Perchin in 1897 as a gift for Czar Nicholas II to give to his wife, Alexandra Feodorovna. Found inside the Coronation Egg is an exact miniature replica of the coronation coach. The Hoof Egg (center), presented by Czarina Alexandra to a good friend, draws from the myth of the centaur, with its cloven-hoof stand. The surprise inside the egg was a miniature portrait of the czarina. The Resurrection Egg (right), made in 1887 for Czar Alexander III for his wife, Maria Feodorovna, is rock crystal with a three-dimensional resurrection scene crafted inside the shell.

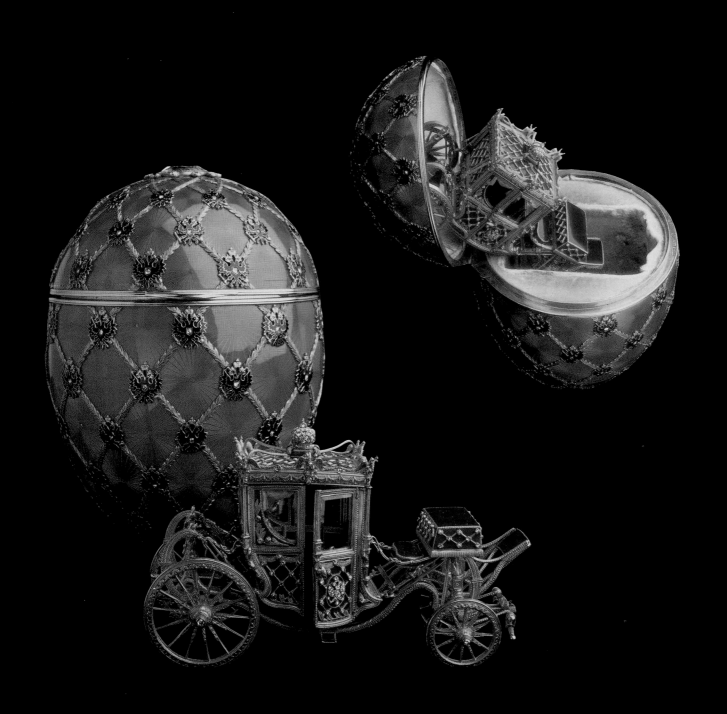

grows from a formal square planter of white chalcedony overlaid with a gold trellis, which, in turn, is surmounted with green enamel laurels swagged with rubies. Flanking the tree at the stand's top four corners are pearl finials; at the base, rubies. But this decorative delight doesn't end with the planter. The planter rests on a two-tiered plinth of nephrite, which, at its four corners, has round columns of nephrite, gold, and pearls that support a "chain fence" of gold leaves enameled a light green and inset with pearls. This remarkable intricacy doesn't preclude the egg of its surprise. At the turn of one of the oranges at the treetop, the crown of the tree lifts, producing a colorful miniature nightingale that sings and hops on its perch, then quickly vanishes once again inside the tree.

Another particularly noteworthy flight of fantasy is the Lilies of the Valley Egg presented by Czar Nicholas II to his mother in 1898. Stamped by Perchin, this delectable egg is eminently feminine, dons a soft pink enamel finish embedded with pearl and diamond Art Nouveau flowers, and is mounted on cabriole legs. The surprise elements in this egg, triggered by a small pearl knob, are miniature portraits of the czar and his two eldest daughters. Each of the portraits is framed in rose diamonds.

Imperial eggs were not always secular. Imagine, a Renaissance-style base slathered with jewels and pearls supporting a rock crystal egg with a superbly crafted, three-dimensional resurrection scene inside its shell. This, one of two eggs with a religious theme made by Fabergé for the court, was presented by Czar Alexander III to his wife, Maria Feodorovna, in 1887 and is thought to be the second egg in the Imperial series. The second egg, given to the dowager empress in 1915, also has an explicit religious message: The surprise within the egg is a miniature triptych of the resurrection.

The Orange Tree Egg (opposite), made in 1911 as an Easter gift for Nicholas II to give to his mother, is larger and more ornate than Fabergé's earlier Imperial eggs, ornamented with carved nephrite (a type of jade), citrine, amethyst, champagne diamonds, sapphires, white chalcedony and, of course, gold and enamel.

Like any other artists, the creative geniuses responsible for conceiving egg designs for the House of Fabergé found themselves influenced by the culture in which they worked. An egg believed to have been presented by Czarina Alexandra to one of her close friends, for instance, contains the fairly conventional surprise feature of a miniature portrait of the czarina herself. But in a diametric departure from convention, the gold laurel-swagged egg rests on cloven hooves — a sophisticated homage to a figure based on the Greek prototype for the centaur in primitive Russian folklore.

While the eggs for which the House of Fabergé gained most acclaim undoubtedly are the Imperial Easter eggs, the shop made a plethora of other eggs of outstanding workmanship and inspired design. Miniature eggs, most measuring less than an inch (2.5 cm) high, were popular as commemorative baubles, which often alluded to Imperial events such as the coronation of Nicholas II in 1896. These small eggs spanned the gamut from restrained elegance to unabashed opulence; some were plain enamel, others were entirely bejeweled. Their minimal size did not mandate any comparable boundaries on creativity. The tiny charms took the shape of a ladybug, a fish, and an acorn, among other figurative forms.

Although most of the best-known Easter eggs were made for Russian royalty, one American was privy to a stellar example of the genre. The distinguished recipient was Consuelo Vanderbilt, Duchess of Marlborough as a result of her marriage to the Duke of Marlborough, Winston Churchill's cousin. Vanderbilt's objet d'art was modeled after the Imperial Serpent Clock Egg, but was executed in blue enamel instead of pink. It is thought that Vanderbilt possibly saw the prototype on her visit to the dowager empress in 1902 and wanted one like it. Both Vanderbilt's egg and the Russian egg were inspired by

Made for Czar Nicholas II to give to his mother in 1898, the Lilies of the Valley Egg (opposite) is finished in pink enamel with pearl and diamond Art Nouveau flowers.

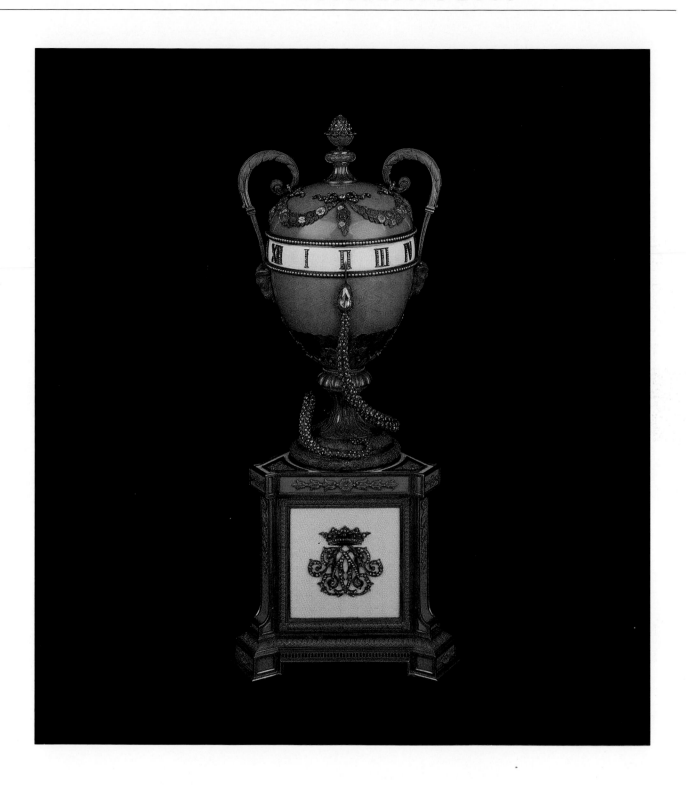

Louis XVI urn clocks. The American egg features numerals made of rose diamonds, which grace a white enamel band delineated by rows of seed pearls. Four colors of gold comprise roses, which form a garland at the top of the egg. A diamond serpent coiling up from the base gauges time with its tongue.

Other eggs, too, were made for wealthy decorative arts aficionados outside the Imperial family. An entire series of eggs was created for the aforementioned heiress Barbara Bazanov Kelch (owner of the Kelch Hen Egg). Several were made for others of privilege — the Emanuel Nobel family (producers of dynamite and Siberian oil), and Prince Felix Yussupov.

After Armand Hammer brought his famed Fabergé treasures to America in the 1930s to sell in his Manhattan gallery, the eggs were owned at various times by such notables as Franklin Delano Roosevelt, J.P. Morgan, King Farouk of Egypt, and shipping magnate Lansdell K. Christie. In the early 1960s, the Imperial eggs caught the fancy of the late American entrepreneur Malcolm S. Forbes. Recalling his introduction to the Fabergé treasures, Forbes once said:

> When very young, I read with horrified fascination an abundantly illustrated volume on World War I. Its chapter about the Russian Revolution and the massacre of the Romanov family included a picture of a Fabergé Imperial Egg to illustrate the pre-war extravagance of Russia's ruler.

By 1979, Forbes had acquired as many Imperial eggs in his collection as the Soviet government itself had retained. In the 1980s, eggs from the *Forbes* magazine collection comprised a major expedition that traveled to museums throughout the United States, providing viewers with a firsthand appreciation of these incredible eggs to which photography only partially does justice.

Known as the Duchess of Marlborough Egg (opposite), this Fabergé creation was modeled after the Imperial Serpent Clock Egg for Consuelo Vanderbilt, Duchess of Marlborough after her visit to the dowager empress in 1902.

From Admiration to Action:

Taking up the Tradition

The Flower Egg

In England, the flower egg is known as the pace egg; in Holland, it's called the sassy egg. Although some variations exist from one culture to another, the basic method of making the flower egg is universal. Decorated entirely of natural, indigenous materials, this classic decorative egg isn't blown, but boiled in an organic dye bath. Imprints of tiny flowers or ferns swathed to the egg with a soft cloth lend the egg its fresh, whimsical charm.

Materials:

- Small ferns and flowers
- Old, soft sheets torn into 12 1-inch × 3-foot (2.5-cm × 1-m) strips
- Old, soft sheets torn into 12 ¼-inch × 18-inch (6-mm × 45-cm) strips, or white twine
- Pot large enough to accommodate 12 eggs
- 36 to 48 onions (or enough to make a deep-colored dye bath)
- 12 white eggs, brought to room temperature

Directions:

Selecting and Binding Organic Matter

For the floral patterns, first harvest any small flowering plant, fern, or dried grass (these produce some of the most interesting designs) found in your area. Select specimens with pleasing shapes, while simultaneously considering how the various plants will compose in the overall design. You may opt for one slightly larger variety to be dominant, for example, or you may wish to have

uniformity of scale. Stars-of-Bethlehem, violets, pansies, redbuds, small roses, dandelions, japonica, hyacinths, and any assortment of delicate wildflowers work equally well for imprinting. Don't ignore flower color, either. Experimentation is the best way to determine which colors will successfully transfer onto the eggshell.

After gathering all of the necessary organic materials, prepare the bindings that will hold them to the egg. Old sheets, softened from wear and wash, are ideal coverings. More porous than new yard goods, they permit maximum penetration of the dye onto the eggs, while their softness minimizes the possibility of any rough fabric edge leaving its own pattern in the dye. Then tear the old sheets into long, narrow strips about 1 inch wide (2.5 cm) by 3 feet long (1 m).

If the sheeting material is sturdy, it also can be used for the outer binder that is tied around the egg to hold the other fabric in place against the plants and eggshell. The binding should be cut into long, narrow strips about ¼ inch (6 mm) wide by 18 inches (45 cm) long. If sheets aren't strong enough, a spool of soft white twine will serve the same purpose.

Preparing the Dye Bath

Any number of natural materials can be used for the dye bath. In England, the yellow flowers of the furze shrub are commonly employed, while Russia favors the pasqueflower for its rich green color. Beet juice or coffee grounds can serve the same function. One of the most traditional substances — and the easiest for most people to lay their hands on — is the humble onion skin.

Both yellow and red onion skins work well as dye baths. Boiled separately, the two onion types produce dyes of different colors. Tossed in the pot together, they create a third hue. However, whatever organic materials you choose, you will probably need to experiment in order to find colors that please you.

To prepare the dye bath, simply boil a pot full of onion skins to produce a fragrant, dark broth. (You need to boil enough water [3 inches or 7.5 cm] so that the eggs will be fully covered when they are being dyed later.) Remove from the stove and cool to room temperature while the eggs are being prepared for the bath.

Preparing the Eggs

When you are ready to start the decorating process, only use eggs that have been brought to room temperature. (Cold eggs tend to crack and are more resistant to color saturation.)

Working on a table or counter, begin by placing the first of your organic materials in the desired position against the shell. Make sure the plant is as flat as possible to achieve the clearest design. Take one of the fabric strips, and beginning with the first plant, pull it over the plant and hold it firmly in place while arranging the next flower in the same manner. Continue positioning and wrapping tightly (but not so tightly that you crack the egg) until all of the materials are pressed against the egg and the egg is completely covered with cloth. Next, give a half twist to the cloth to ensure that both ends of the egg are fully covered. No bare eggshell should be exposed.

Once the egg is wrapped, take a strip of the ¼-inch (6-mm) binding fabric (or twine) and wrap it around the egg once more to secure.

The prepared eggs are finally ready for the onion-dye bath. Return the pot of onion skins to the stove top; the onion skins need not be removed before adding the eggs. (If you decide to use a smaller pot, say a 4-quart [4-l] saucepan, place no more than 3 to 5 eggs in the pan at a time.) After submerging the eggs in the broth, cook them rather slowly — at a simmer for at least 8 minutes. The goal is twofold: to hard-boil the eggs and to absorb as much of the color bath as possible.

When the eggs are done, carefully remove them from the pot with a large slotted spoon, and toss aside any onion skins that might be stuck to the surface. Then place the eggs in a bowl of room-temperature water and wait for them to cool. For faster results, keep replacing the water with fresh tap water.

By this time, the wrappings should have loosened and fallen off the egg. If not, untie the binders and remove the cloth.

Pysanky

Decorating the Ukrainian wax-resist eggs known as pysanky requires the proper materials, time, patience, and practice. But the results are worth the effort.

Notes:

- It is suggested that beginners limit the number of dyes they use to 6.
- Remember that aniline dyes are chemicals that will render the eggs inedible.
- Do not erase your penciled pattern; if you do, the wax will not take.

Materials:

- A table surface covered with a bottom layer of newspaper and a layer of tissue
- 2 ounces (56 g) of beeswax (not candle wax or paraffin)
- Tin can (resting in a hot pan of water)
- Half a black crayon or ½ teaspoon (2.5 ml) black shoe polish
- Small paper cups

- Pencil

- Fresh white raw eggs at room temperature, which have been washed with a solution of one part white vinegar to four parts tepid water, then gently patted dry

- 2 or 3 various-sized kistky (a funnel attached to a stick), the writing tool used for scooping the wax, which is then heated and drawn across the egg in the desired patterns

- Candle for heating the kistky

- 6 tablespoons

- Aniline dyes: yellow, orange, red, green, black, and blue. (Mix these dyes with boiling water according to package instructions and allow to cool in widemouthed jars.)

- Small can of clear gloss varnish

- An egg holder made from wood or cardboard into which small nails have been driven through the top to form a triangular nest in which to hold each egg as it dries

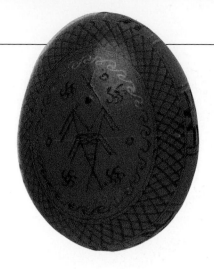

Directions:

Melt 2 ounces (56 g) of beeswax in a tin can placed in a hot pan of water (not boiling). As the wax melts, add half of a black crayon or ½ teaspoon (2.5 ml) of black shoe polish. After the beeswax turns black, pour it into small paper cups and allow it to cool. When ready to draw on wax designs, simply peel back the paper cup and use the cake of dark wax to fill the kistky.

Starting vertically from its top, *lightly* draw a line with a pencil all around the egg until you are back where you began. Then draw another line around the egg's center, or equator. Now draw two diagonal lines, which will bisect each of the four sections created by the first two lines. You should have an egg that's divided into eight equal sections by the time you finish.

Now fill the kistky with the wax and make a small dot at the center point of the egg. Tracing the pencil guideline made in step one, create your first design in one of the eight areas closest to the center point, then repeat the exact design at an equidistance from the center in the remaining eight segments.

Place the egg on a tablespoon and dip it into one of the aniline dye baths. Leave the egg in the bath for 5 to 10 minutes, or until it has reached the desired color. Remove the egg and pat it dry, but don't rub it.

Onto the colored egg, make your next wax design, dip into the next dye, and repeat the process.

Continue in this way until all of the desired dyes have been included. A recommended dyeing order runs from light to dark: yellow, green, blue, orange, red, black. Always save the black dye for last, and allow the egg a longer time to absorb the dye — you may need to let it remain in the black bath up to 30 minutes.

Allow 15 minutes for the egg to dry before removing the wax. To do this, hold the egg by a candle flame and move it slowly back and forth until it appears wet. Then wipe the wax off with a soft cotton cloth. Don't hold the egg over the candle directly, as the carbon will blacken the design.

After melting and wiping all the wax from the egg, wipe the egg again using a mild cleaning fluid to ensure the removal of all wax and blemishes.

Varnish the eggs by applying a thin coat of varnish to each one. Then place the eggs on the homemade egg rack to dry for several hours.

Every few months, turn your pysanky over to assure that the contents dry evenly.

Blown Eggs

Many traditions of egg decorating call for blown eggs. (Finished pysanky can be blown, if desired, after the varnish has been applied and dried.) The process is simple but takes practice.

Using a long pin, make two holes in both ends of the egg — a tiny hole at the top, and a larger one (about ⅛ inch [3 mm]) at the bottom. Manipulate the pin inside the egg to pierce the yolk, then shake the egg vigorously to blend the contents. Now blow through the smaller hole to push the contents out of the larger hole. Rinse the shell immediately after the insides have been blown, and allow the egg to dry.

INDEX

PRINCIPAL PHOTOGRAPHY BY:

JOHN GRUEN, New York, pp:
6 (lower left), 8, 18, 58, 59, 60, 61, 62, 63, 64, 65, 66, 67, 70, 94, 95, 98, 99, 100, 103, 104, 105

RICHARD TODD, Los Angeles, pp:
2, 3, 6 (left to right), 9, 13, 14, 15, 16, 17, 20, 22, 23, 32, 36 (left, center, right), 37, 38, 39, 40, 41, 42, 43, 44, 45, 46, 47, 48, 49, 50, 51, 53, 54, 55, 56, 57, 77

With other contributions from:

Forbes Magazine Collection, pp. 79; photos by H. Peter Curran, pp. 80 (top left), 83, 87, 88, 90, 92; photos by Larry Stein, pp. 76, 80 (lower page), 81, 86

Courtesy of the Balzekas Museum of Lithuanian Culture, Chicago, IL, photos by Ed Mankus, pp. 11 from the collection of Frances Drwal; eggs by Linda Markus, pp. 75

Collection of the Lithuanian Folk Art Institute, eggs by Jouzas Jasiunas, Detroit, MI, pp. 58, 73

Monika Manns, pp. 109

Susanna Pashko, Envision, pp. 27

Courtesy of the Romanian Folk Art Museum, Evanston, IL, photo by Ed Mankus, pp. 25

Carol Simowitz, pp. 24 (center), 28, 29 (lower left)

Courtesy of Williams-Sonoma pp. 29 (upper right), 33

About the Author

Candace Ord Manroe, interior design and arts editor of *Country Home* magazine, is a native Texan who now resides in Des Moines, Iowa, with her two children, Meagan and Drew.

Her free-lance stories on art and decorative art, architecture, and design have appeared in national magazines, including *Architectural Digest, Better Homes and Gardens,* and New York Times Group and Hearst publications. She is the author of *Shaker* and *The Horse Companion* (autumn 1992).

A journalism graduate of the University of Texas at Austin, she is completing graduate studies in English literature at Drake University.

She spends her free time riding her horse and writing poetry.